★★★★★ *The* ★★★★★
CIVIL WAR
150

An Essential To-Do List for the 150th Anniversary

Civil War Trust

Garry E. Adelman, Editor
James Campi, Contributing Editor
Mary Koik, Contributing Editor
Nicholas Redding, Contributing Editor
Daniel Schwarz, Contributing Editor

LYONS PRESS
Guilford, Connecticut
An imprint of Globe Pequot Press

To buy books in quantity for corporate use
or incentives, call **(800) 962–0973**
or e-mail **premiums@GlobePequot.com**.

Lyons Press is an imprint of Globe Pequot Press.

Text design: Sheryl Kober
Layout artist: Melissa Evarts
Project editor: Kristen Mellitt

Library of Congress Cataloging-in-Publication Data is available on file.

ISBN 978-0-7627-7207-0

Printed in the United States of America

10 9 8 7 6

Contents

Civil War 150 Essays

Area Maps

Foreword

By James Lighthizer, President, Civil War Trust

A century and a half has passed since a bloodless artillery exchange in Charleston Harbor ignited the most bloody and tragic conflict in our nation's history. For four long years, armies in blue and gray roamed the countryside, clashing in more than 10,000 battles and skirmishes that defined us as a nation and sounded the death knell of slavery. When the guns fell silent in the spring of 1865, more than 600,000 Americans had lost their lives.

Despite the passage of time, Americans of all ages remain fascinated with the Civil War. Some are interested because they had a teacher who sparked a curiosity that resulted in a lifelong passion for history. Others are among the more than 100 million Americans that can trace their ancestry back to someone who served in the conflict. Still more are held spellbound by the writings and diaries left behind by those who lived through the fateful struggle.

Regardless of the reason, those of us who are interested in the Civil War find ourselves, almost inevitably, driven to visit the sites where the war occurred. There is something about the human condition that makes us seek out the places we have read about, to touch the artifacts or enter the buildings associated with that history.

This book is about feeding that insatiable craving so many of us have to experience the Civil War. In these pages, we describe 150 things the reader can see or do to learn more about the war that pitted brother against brother and family against family. We recommend the reader visit such famous battlefields as Gettysburg and Vicksburg, hold a Civil War Minie ball, attend a reenactment, maybe even take a bite of Civil War hardtack.

In some instances, you don't even need to leave the comfort of your own home. You can curl up with one of Pulitzer Prize–winning author Bruce Catton's many memorable books, browse an extensive collection of Civil War photographs on the Library of Congress website, or enjoy the movies *Gone With the Wind* and *Glory* from the comfort of your favorite sofa. Regardless of what you choose, be sure to have fun with it!

For us at the Civil War Trust, we hope this book will also spark interest in preserving the hallowed battlegrounds where the Civil War occurred. As America enters the 150th anniversary of the conflict, many Civil War battlefields are on the verge of being lost forever. Some places, like Chantilly and Salem Church, are mere shadows of once extensive battlegrounds. You can learn more about these endangered battlegrounds by visiting our website at Civilwar.org.

I encourage you to engage in as many of these 150 activities as possible. Enjoy them. Be inspired by them. Encourage a friend and family member to participate. And please help the Civil War Trust preserve the experience for future generations of Americans.

Introduction

$\mathcal{O}$ne afternoon in 2009, a tree fell across the tracks and I was stuck on my commuter train for more than three hours. That's when this project began in earnest. After a brief conversation with the Civil War Trust's Jim Campi about doing a Civil War sesquicentennial book, I set out to create 150 "listings" of things people might do to commemorate the anniversary.

But by the time the train started moving, I had already listed more than 340 essential activities. After another brainstorming session, the list had swollen to more than one thousand, and I realized it was necessary to split the project into a larger web-based piece and a book of more limited scope. The former includes one listing for each of the more than 1,400 days of the sesquicentennial, while the print edition you now hold in your hands underwent a most painful of editing processes. How could climbing Shy's Hill at Nashville or visiting the Manassas Museum be removed from a list of essential activities when they are, indeed, essential? Does not Fraley Field at Shiloh or Richmond's Hollywood Cemetery deserve its own listing? How could I include the death site of the Gallant Pelham while leaving off the death site of Turner Ashby? In the end, the task of winnowing the list down to just 150 proved to be frustrating and painful—frankly, it was all but impossible.

I am, therefore, particularly aware that not everyone will agree with the content of the list. Blame me. My ultimate goal was to assemble 150 things that every Civil War enthusiast should do encompassing a topical and geographic variety that would appeal to an array of people, and I hope I succeeded. Although I have spent more than twenty years visiting Civil War sites, I found that I have only completed 131 of the 150 items. I have some work to do!

For the real enthusiasts out there, we are thoroughly covering the complete range of to-do listings on our web-based piece and will highlight one listing each day on our website throughout the sesquicentennial.

I encourage you to visit www.civilwar.org/list and begin working on the extended checklist.

While I am eager to accept the responsibility for any omissions in this book, I am equally anxious to give credit to the many people who made this book possible. Without them, I doubt that it would have been completed at any point during the sesquicentennial, never mind in time for its outset. Civil War Trust intern Daniel Schwarz had the unenviable task of turning my initial thoughts into actual listings with descriptions. For months, he built out the initial list to include more than 1,200 listings. My Civil War Trust colleagues James Campi, Mary Koik, and Nicholas Redding all helped to build out, edit, and stylize the listings in short order. This was no small task; in some cases, trying to describe the essence of these places in eighty to two hundred words was as difficult as paring the list down to 150 in the first place. Tracey McIntire, David Wiemer, Clayton Butler, and Katherine Stinson all helped with research, writing, and photo selection duties. Erin Wetherley had perhaps the most frustrating task of all—making maps of the sections when I didn't even know what I wanted on the maps. She was more patient than I would have been in her place, and her input made the maps far better. An advance thank you goes out to the Civil War Trust web team—Rob Shenk, Jim Drey, Wendy Woodford, and Doug Ullman—which has already begun helping with the larger To-Do List project. Bill Vodra, Ron Cogswell, Frank DeLuca, and Hal Jespersen all provided helpful comments that ultimately made the list better. My former colleagues at History Associates, under the direction of Civil War honcho Halley Fehner, made numerous key saves and suggestions right near the end. She was assisted by Robert Colby, Matthew Morrill, and Andrew Simpson.

I sincerely thank the following for providing the lion's share of the photographs for this book: Civil War Trust, Library of Congress, National Archives, Rob Shenk, and Wikimedia Commons. I also used many of my own photographs. Other photographers' credits accompany their photographs.

From the first discussion of the book, the staff at Globe Pequot has shown great interest in this project. Katie Benoit, Steve Culpepper, and Kristen Mellitt, in particular, were enthusiastic partners in working with this Civil War nerd on a project so personal in nature. I also want to thank our partners in preservation without whom there would be none of these sites to visit in the first place.

Lastly, my wife, Jennifer, has not only tolerated my very substantial Civil War obsession for more than a decade but also made helpful design-related comments along the way. She watched patiently as I put Civil War books next to our sons when they were less than two hours old and knows that they will be dragged to many of the sites in this book in the coming years. Her past and future understanding deserves my greatest gratitude.

Garry Adelman
Director of History and Education,
Civil War Trust
Washington, D.C.
January 11, 2011

THE BASICS: BOOKS TO BULLETS

*T*he Civil War permeates American society in so many ways. More than 100 million people have Civil War ancestors; politicians revere and exploit its history with great frequency. Writers churn out more books on the Civil War than on any other American history topic.

Although there are Civil War–related sites in most every state, most Americans do not live within 200 miles of a major Civil War battlefield. And when enthusiasts do make pilgrimages to Civil War sites, sometimes over significant distances, the experience can be heightened by covering the basics in advance. For many people, the eventual trip to Charleston, South Carolina, is far more important after having seen the movie *Glory*. For others, touring the sites of Union General Ulysses S. Grant's Overland Campaign will have deeper meaning after having read Bruce Catton's *Grant Takes Command*. When visiting the Shenandoah Valley, having donned a Civil War uniform and carried a gun for even just ten minutes will make people stand in awe of Confederate General Stonewall Jackson's "foot cavalry," which marched more than 640 miles in forty-eight days in 1862. And standing on a battlefield such as that at Perryville, Kentucky, learning on that battlefield, and pondering what happened there is far more powerful if you were involved in its preservation.

The time is now. Start checking these items off your Civil War 150 Checklist and your Civil War experiences, whatever these may be, will be more profound and more fun.

HOLD A MINIE BALL IN YOUR HAND

Why? Once you have felt a Minie ball in your hand, you can begin to get a sense of its devastating potential.

Description: When you hold a Minie ball, you experience a visceral connection with the common Civil War soldier, who routinely loaded them into his rifled muskets in the heat of battle to fire at his fellow Americans. As the most common Civil War projectile, its destructive power is readily apparent. Feel the Minie ball, and imagine yourself on a battlefield with thousands of them flying around you. Go to a Civil War antique store or a Civil War battlefield bookstore to find one.

Holding a Minie ball in your hand, just once, can foster a better understanding of the war.

Don a Uniform or Period Dress

Why? *To take a walk in the shoes of Civil War participants.*

Description: You'll feel closer to and get a better understanding of any historical period by dressing as they did back then. And nothing distinguished the armies of North and South as did their uniforms: the Blue and the Gray. Assuming the look of a soldier or 1860s civilian will enable you to immerse yourself in their world and lose yourself in what many reenactors call the "period rush." Contact a reenactment/historical unit in your area for information on obtaining uniforms or civilian dress. Try a loaner before you decide if this is something you want to invest in. Whether it's buying uniforms or making your own, reenactment groups are usually set up to help you do that. Often, groups will include one or two people who volunteer as seamstresses. For a small fee and purchase of the material, these helpful historical recreationists can have you dressing, and feeling, like it's 1861.

Whether soldier or civilian, there's much to be said for dressing for the part.

Take a Bite of Hardtack

Why? *If you want an example of what the common soldier had to endure for sustenance during the Civil War, you have to bite and taste hardtack.*

Description: Hardtack is a simple type of cracker or biscuit, made from flour, water, and salt. Cheap to make, forever lasting, and easy to box and transport, it was not necessarily beloved by the troops. The easiest way for you to try hardtack is to find a recipe and cook some. Try it, but watch out for broken teeth—if it doesn't hurt at least a little, you didn't make it right! Once you've had a bite, imagine hardtack was the only thing available to eat for days, weeks, and even months at a time, and you may come closer to understanding another one of the hardships borne by the average Civil War soldier.

Hardtack from Atlanta Area, 1862
T. T. Wentworth, Jr. Collection
The standard Army ration of bread was issued as hardtack, which was supposed to have a longer shelf life than regular bread. The crackers were often so wormy that ...ders nicknamed them "worm castles."

While most hardtack made today is far softer than its Civil War counterpart, you should still be careful taking a bite!

GO TO A CIVIL WAR ROUND TABLE MEETING

Why? *Expand your horizons about various Civil War subjects, and socialize with others who share your passion for the Civil War.*

Description: Most Civil War Round Tables, or CWRTs, meet on a monthly basis, and each meeting covers a different facet of Civil War study. Attend a meeting and you will not only learn new things about the Civil War, but you will come into contact with others who share your love and passion for the war. Civil War Round Tables exist in most major (and many minor) cities; the best way to find one near you is simply to do a search online. Round Table meetings feature a different keynote speaker every month and usually include announcements of local Civil War events or preservation and fundraising opportunities.

WHY DO THIS STUFF?

Why does the Civil War arouse such strong emotions in people? Why do we drive hundreds of miles or more to see battlefields, houses, museums, and other related Civil War sites? Why do we study Civil War battles and events in such detail? Why are we still stirred by these events that took place nearly 150 years ago? Why do we regard battlefields as hallowed ground?

Photo by Debra Pittenturf

War, perhaps more than anything else people can do, brings forth the best and worst of human behavior. A battlefield can invoke a human encounter with life and death in a way that words or pictures cannot. Books, videos, and movies may fill in as noble substitutes, and are important tools to help us understand the Civil War. But there's nothing more powerful than the authenticity of the real thing. We stand awestruck at these places, as we try to learn what happened there, and we are moved in some way—whether saddened, angered, confused, uplifted, impassioned, or enriched.

Today, thanks to the efforts of many, you still have the opportunity to walk upon battlefields at Manassas, Shiloh, Antietam, Gettysburg, Vicksburg, Fredericksburg, Chickamauga, and seemingly countless others. You can drive west of Petersburg and see where Grant accepted Lee's surrender. You can stand atop Lookout Mountain and ponder the impossibility of seizing the height. You can visit the room where President Lincoln breathed his last, and you can literally touch the same trees, rocks, and door handles while gazing up at the same sun, moon, and stars as the brave souls involved in the conflict so long ago. Call it a history lesson, call it time travel, call it whatever you'd like. In the end, *doing,* as opposed to simply learning, is deeply meaningful.

★ ★ ★

READ A BRUCE CATTON BOOK

Why? *You simply can't call yourself a real Civil War enthusiast without reading a Bruce Catton book.*

Description: Catton was a celebrated journalist and historian of the Civil War who won a 1954 Pulitzer Prize in the history category for *A Stillness at Appomattox.* The book is a compelling account of the final year of the Civil War. Specializing in character-based histories, Catton breathed life into sometimes-routine historical factoids. Shelby Foote is considered his closest rival in terms of pure storytelling ability, but in a prodigious line of Civil War historians, Catton is considered by many to be the greatest of all. His work has become required reading for all true Civil War aficionados.

Read and Watch *Gone With the Wind*

Why? Gone with the Wind *must be the most beloved Civil War novel of all time, and the movie remains the highest-grossing domestic film in U.S. history when adjusted for inflation.*

Description: Margaret Mitchell's *Gone With the Wind*, first published in May 1936, is one of the best-known American novels as well as a Pulitzer Prize winner. Her story is set in Georgia, during the Civil War and Reconstruction, and it follows the experiences of Scarlett O'Hara, the spoiled daughter of a wealthy plantation owner. The novel was the source for the 1939 movie of the same name, which featured legendary movie stars Clark Gable, Vivien Leigh, Leslie Howard, Olivia de Havilland, and Hattie McDaniel. Today, the movie still ranks as one of the greatest of all time. In addition, at more than three and a half hours it was the longest American sound film ever created at the time it was made. With the book and the movie, readers and viewers alike are transported to the Old South and see it swept away, gone with the wind.

See the Movie *Glory*

Why? Glory *is among the best Civil War movies (if not* the *best ever made). Watching it, you will learn about the pivotal role that blacks played in helping to win the war for the Union.*

Description: *Glory* (1989) is based upon the experiences of Colonel Robert Gould Shaw, the twenty-five-year-old son of Boston abolitionists who volunteered to command the all-black 54th Regiment of the Massachusetts Volunteer Infantry. The movie is based in part on the books *Lay This Laurel* by Lincoln Kirstein and *One Gallant Rush* by Peter Burchard. It also draws from Shaw's letters.

The movie follows the story from the creation of the regiment through its training and early fighting, and culminates with its final assault on Fort Wagner near Charleston, South Carolina. The regiment's incredible bravery turned a terrible defeat into a symbolic victory that finally brought recognition to black soldiers and helped turn the tide of the war. Like all Civil War movies, there are some problems with historical details, but in general this film shows a greater deference to history than most. Furthermore, the movie offers fine performances from the likes of Matthew Broderick, Denzel Washington (who won the Oscar for Best Supporting Actor), Morgan Freeman, Cary Elwes, and Andre Braugher. Directed by Edward Zwick, it is an unforgettable drama.

Watch Ken Burns' Miniseries *The Civil War*

Why? *This series is arguably the best and most important Civil War documentary.*

Description: Ken Burns' *The Civil War* first aired on PBS on five consecutive nights in 1990. Some forty million viewers watched it during the initial broadcast, which made it the most watched program ever shown on PBS. The importance of this documentary is significant yet immeasurable. Visitation at Civil War battlefields and memorial sites skyrocketed in the summer after its initial airing. The documentary was digitally remastered on the twelfth anniversary of its release, and a book that accompanies the documentary has also been released. The numerous mistakes in the series do little to detract from the vast amount of Civil War knowledge you will acquire by watching it. If you are a teacher, you will benefit from the time-coded descriptions that the PBS website offers of every topic covered in each episode, which allow you to teach a one- or two-day lesson around specific clips.

PRESERVE A BATTLEFIELD

Why? *The chance to save these unique resources is rapidly disappearing and anyone passionate about the Civil War should take part in the fight to save hallowed ground.*

Description: Battlefields are part of our national heritage—scenes of struggle and sacrifice where American soldiers lost their lives. Preserving battlefields allows future generations to learn of the struggles of soldiers and appreciate the hard-won freedoms they enjoy. There are many other benefits as well. Understanding military campaigns and battles is crucial to comprehending the other aspects of the Civil War. In addition, preserved land can satisfy the insatiable craving for authenticity that books and movies (and most certainly developed land) simply cannot. The battlefields were there during the war and there is no substitute for standing there

Battlefields face constant threats to their preservation, such as this adjacent mining operation at Cedar Creek. Photo by Larry Solvey

yourself. Visiting battlefields allows you to experience a visceral connection with the soldiers who fought and died there. Joshua Lawrence Chamberlain, returning to the Gettysburg battlefield years after his regiment's heroic exploits, noted, "In great deeds, something abides. On great fields something stays. Forms change and pass; bodies disappear, but spirits linger." Every visitor to a Civil War battlefield has experienced these feelings in one way or another.

Numerous organizations, including the Civil War Trust, help save battlefields. Visit the Trust's website, make a donation, or get involved!

Get a Kid Interested in the Civil War

Why? It is up to future generations to continue preserving Civil War battlefields in this country, and to keep the spirit and memory of that great struggle alive.

Description: It's rewarding to foster interest among the young, and if it's about a subject you love, all the better! Family vacations, field trips, movies, books, and costumes (kids love the blue and gray caps) are just some of the interactive ways to introduce the Civil War to the younger generation. Every child is different, and you will have to find the best approach for the kids whom you know. They may not understand why you are taking them to Chickamauga now, but they will hopefully appreciate it in the future. Always remember that you are informing, and perhaps even inspiring, American's next generation.

Whether as a student, spectator, or participant, you have the ability to foster in young people a lifelong and rewarding passion for Civil War history.
Photo by Jason Morrison

Take a Civil War Driving Tour

Why? *Gain a better geographical understanding of a Civil War campaign and spend some quality time with your family and friends in the process.*

Description: From our perspective, there are few better ways to spend time than by taking a Civil War driving tour. The "Civil War Trails" signage in several states can direct you to numerous driving tours that are each worth a try. Try Grant's Overland Campaign through Northern Virginia, or spend a day exploring the Civil War legacy of a specific town (Lynchburg, Richmond, Front Royal, Knoxville, Chattanooga, and Atlanta are just a few examples). These self-guided driving tours allow you to move at your own pace and stay longer at some stops without being left behind by a tour-bus driver. Driving tours also give you the opportunity to hop on or off the given route at different points at your convenience. As you tour, remember that Stonewall Jackson's Valley Campaign, Robert E. Lee's retreat to Appomattox, or General Sherman's advance through the Carolinas is infinitely more enjoyable to experience in your car than it ever was for the hard-marching troops.

Experience a Reenactment

Why? *You will see the smoke, hear the roar of cannon fire, smell the powder, and get a glimpse into the incredible spectacle that was a Civil War battle.*

Description: Good Civil War reenactments are carefully planned efforts to faithfully re-create the events of a particular battle or action. Engagements range from the extremely small, with only a handful of participants, to full scale, in which thousands participate. Go to a reenactment to see uniformed men marching stoutly in their lines, to hear commanders try to shout their orders above the cacophony of rifles and artillery being fired, and to comprehend the mass confusion of battle.

Many people are visual learners, so by seeing a Civil War battle, people come away with a fuller understanding than they would have gained otherwise. Of course, no cannonballs are flying, no bullets are whizzing through the air, and no one is getting killed, but it nevertheless provides a real glimpse at what a Civil War battle might have looked like. Many reenactments also feature extensive encampments through which you can walk and interact with living historians between battles. Conduct an online search for locations and times of these events.

Small or large, a reenactment is something you must experience.
Photo by Will Hart, courtesy of HISTORY™

PICK UP A CANNONBALL OR SHELL

Why? Once you've picked up a cannonball or shell, you will have a small idea of what soldiers must have felt every time one of these things was sent hurling their way.

Description: You can find shells or cannonballs in several places—at antique stores, in museums, at the Civil War national parks, and on display at some Civil War reenactments. It's more than worthwhile to badger the antique dealer into letting you pick up a projectile. After you feel its weight, just imagine a host of these plowing or exploding through a line of soldiers.

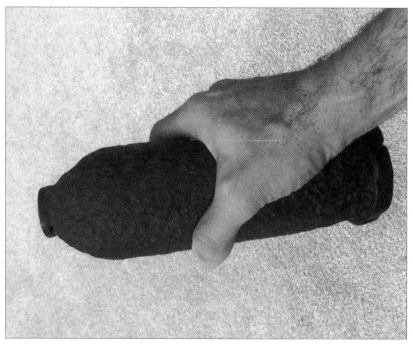

Pick up a projectile, such as this ten-pound Confederate Parrott shell, and imagine it flying toward you and then exploding.

FIRE A CIVIL WAR GUN

Why? Without loading, firing, and being engulfed in the smoke from a Civil War rifle, you cannot fully understand a Civil War firefight.

Description: Learning to load and fire a Civil War rifle is an eye-opening experience for anyone interested in what life was like for the average soldier. If a good soldier could fire three shots in a minute, then 57 seconds of every minute had to be spent furiously loading and reloading. This is fundamentally important to understanding what was asked of the average Civil War private. And once you see the smoke that just one of these rifles produces every time it is fired, you will better appreciate the very real problems that smoke caused on Civil War battlefields. Join a reenactment group, go to a reenactment, or participate in events such as those held at Pamplin Historical Park in Petersburg, Virginia, where you will be taught the *nine-step* firing procedure. Once you load and fire a rifle, feel the kick, and carry that heavy beast around for even thirty minutes, you can be assured that you will have a far better understanding of and appreciation for the principal instrument of the Civil War.

Pamplin Historical Park is among the places where you can learn how to load and fire a Civil War gun.

THE GATHERING STORM

The Civil War did not begin overnight; a series of events and personalities led the nation to war. Numerous conflicts exacerbated sectional differences, particularly over the spread and continuation of slavery as new territories sought statehood.

Horace Greeley, an editor of the *New York Tribune,* is credited with coining the term "Bleeding Kansas" to describe the violent conflict that emerged in the Kansas Territory and the western frontier towns of Missouri between 1854 and 1858. With the Kansas-Nebraska Act, Congress had determined that popular sovereignty would determine whether Kansas would enter the Union as a free state or a slave state. Activists from both sides rushed to Kansas, sparking violence so intense that two governments, each with its own constitution, were briefly in place. On January 29, 1861, a month after South Carolina seceded,

John C. Calhoun.

Kansas was admitted to the Union as a free state. Check out the Freedom's Frontier National Heritage Area for information, events, and on-site interpretation.

As the events of Bleeding Kansas were swirling, a little-known Illinois lawyer was making a name for himself through a series of orations outlining the evils of slavery and decrying the violence caused by "popular sovereignty," which had caused so much trouble in Kansas. Although he lost his race for the U.S. Senate, Abraham Lincoln gained enough notoriety to emerge as a contender for the Republican presidential nomination in 1860. When Lincoln won the 1860 election, the South began carrying through on its threat to secede from the Union. In December, inspired by a long association with the principle of nullification of federal laws by dissenting states—famously championed by John C. Calhoun in the 1830s—delegates voted 169 to 0 to declare "that the Union now subsisting between South Carolina and other states under the name of the 'United States of America' is hereby dissolved."

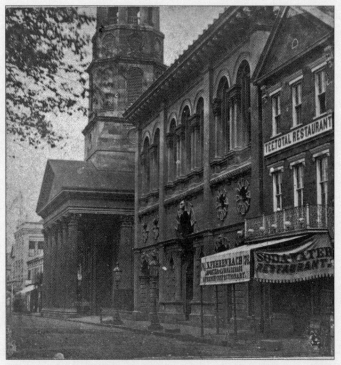

Secession Hall, at center.

Don't Do This List Alone

Why? It's fun and more meaningful when you have a companion or a group that shares your love for Civil War history.

Description: Hiking and visiting battlefields, going to museums, participating in Round Table meetings, and debating the endless facets of the Civil War are all so much livelier when there is a friend along for the ride. If your "Civil War buddy" shares your passion, you can learn more from each other than would have ever been possible alone. Buddies challenge one another. Every time your buddy gets interested in a new Civil War topic, you're going to hear about it too, and before you know it you'll both be visiting the site and discussing the topic on the Internet!

Whether you see a movie or cross a battlefield stream, all Civil War–related experiences are more meaningful when shared with others.

READ *BATTLE CRY OF FREEDOM*

Why? This is the one book that anybody wanting to learn about the Civil War must read.

Description: For more than twenty years, there has been one book that every Civil War buff or novice must own: *Battle Cry of Freedom,* by James M. McPherson. Loaded with new interpretations and information that serve to challenge old thinking, *Battle Cry of Freedom* is the must-own one-volume history of the Civil War. The book is a fast-paced and detailed narrative that explores all the political, social, and military events that led to the Civil War—the war in Mexico, the Dred Scott decision, the Lincoln-Douglas debates, Bleeding Kansas, John Brown's raid on Harpers Ferry—and then brilliantly chronicles the Civil War itself, including the surrender at Appomattox.

The book's title refers to the way both Northerners and Southerners viewed the Civil War: The Confederate states all seceded to protect the freedom of self-determination and self-government on which this nation was founded in 1776, while the North fought to defend the Union. Ultimately, however, the North would be forced to come to grips with the real cause of the war—slavery—and emancipation soon became a second major goal of the war. This "new birth of freedom," which Lincoln talked about in the Gettysburg Address, is no doubt the proudest legacy of the Civil War.

VISIT A CONFEDERATE CEMETERY

Why? *You honor the final resting place of the Southern soldiers who died in service throughout the war.*

Description: Hundreds of Civil War cemeteries exist throughout the states that constituted the Confederacy, and they vary greatly in size and stature. Some of these cemeteries are smaller and notable primarily for someone (or something) specific. For example, the family cemetery at Ellwood, on the Wilderness Battlefield, is well-known as the resting place of Stonewall Jackson's arm. A few cemeteries, on the other hand, are massive. Hollywood Cemetery in Richmond, Virginia, with its pathways overlooking the James River, contains the graves of Jefferson Davis and 18,000 Confederate soldiers. Blandford Cemetery in Petersburg is even larger and is

The McGavock Confederate Cemetery in Franklin, Tennessee, contains more than 1,300 graves.

renowned for beautiful stained-glass windows in the adjacent Old Blandford Church. Oakland Cemetery in Atlanta, Georgia, is the final resting place of some 6,900 Confederate soldiers.

The sheer number of Confederate cemeteries and the number of soldiers interred therein underscore the incredible Southern commitment to its cause. Nearly half of military-aged Southern males were killed or wounded in the war, and the cemeteries created as their last resting places offer permanent testament to what that number truly means. No matter how grand or how humble, they all have one important thing in common: They are first and foremost the final resting place for the Confederate soldiers who gave their lives for cause and comrades on their native soil. By taking the time out to go and visit one of these Confederate cemeteries, and reflecting on that sacrifice, you can pay the ultimate honor to the soldiers, sailors, and others who lost their lives.

STROLL THROUGH A NATIONAL CEMETERY

Why? *You honor the Union soldiers who died in the service of their country.*

Description: The first National Cemeteries in the United States were dedicated during the Civil War, and there are scores of them around the country, usually adjacent to or within the grounds of major battlefields. Some of the National Cemeteries are small, while others are grimly expansive. And each is unique and notable for one reason or another. The Soldiers National Cemetery at Gettysburg, Pennsylvania, is where President Lincoln delivered his Gettysburg Address, while Arlington National Cemetery in Washington, D.C., was once the estate of Confederate General Robert E. Lee. Chattanooga's and Fredericksburg's are absolutely massive and provide excellent views. Ball's Bluff in Leesburg, Virginia, and

The National Cemetery at Elmira, New York.

Battleground in Washington, D.C., are small but meaningful. Shiloh's is stunningly beautiful while Antietam has the largest statue of a soldier you are likely to see.

Other federal cemeteries may be less well known, but are no less interesting, and are certainly worth a visit, for they all have one crucial thing in common: They serve as the last resting place for the Union troops who gave their lives for cause and comrades. More than one in ten Union soldiers was killed or died of disease in the service of their country. By taking the time to go and visit one of these graveyards, and to meditate on the thousands of souls resting there, you pay the ultimate honor to the soldiers, sailors, and others who lost their lives over the course of the Civil War. Most National Cemeteries display the text of the Gettysburg Address and text from the Mexican War–era poem, *The Bivouac of the Dead*, on iron signage.

Experience a Battlefield Illumination Event

Why? *An illumination is visually stunning and by going you will honor those who gave their lives to the nation's epic event.*

Description: Watching an illumination luminary on a battlefield, you can picture just how many people died in the various actions of the war. At these events, each soldier's grave or each soldier that died at that place is honored with a luminary candle. At some events, "Taps" is played every thirty minutes in memory of the fallen soldiers and a quiet hush falls over the area for a time. Many national parks and other Civil War sites hold illumination events at some point during the year, and if you are given the opportunity, stay long enough to watch the flames extinguish—the parallels between the candle and a soldier's life are abundantly evident.

Antietam's annual Memorial Illumination is unforgettable. Photo by Chad Keener

See *The Great Locomotive Chase*

Why? It's a great movie based on a fascinating, actual event—the April 1862 Union theft of a Confederate locomotive in Georgia.

Description: The 1956 Disney film about the Great Locomotive Chase stars Fess Parker as James J. Andrews, who led a group of Federal soldiers from Ohio behind Confederate lines, where they stole a Confederate train and took it back to Union lines. In the process, they wrecked railroad tracks, burned bridges, and cut telegraph lines. Eventually, these men were captured and some of them were even executed as spies. But some of them became the first recipients of the Medal of Honor.

Appreciate the Crater Scene in *Cold Mountain*

Why? *The beginning of the film contains the best depiction of the Battle of the Crater.*

Description: Film can be a very powerful medium, and when its subject matter is handled properly it can drive home its message better than almost anything else. The first few minutes of the film *Cold Mountain* depicts the Battle of the Crater, which took place on July 30, 1864. See the horrors and trauma of that particular battle and you may well concur with General Grant's assessment that the battle was "the saddest affair I have witnessed in the war."

SEE THE FLANK ATTACK IN *GODS AND GENERALS*

Why? *This is your one opportunity to see one of the most famous flank attacks of the Civil War.*

Description: This film is based on the best-selling historical novel of the same name by Jeff Shaara, and it covers select Eastern Theater events of the Civil War before the Battle of Gettysburg. It primarily follows Stonewall Jackson from the Virginia Military Institute to his wounding at the Battle of Chancellorsville. While the movie has received mixed reviews from Civil War enthusiasts, Jackson's Flank Attack at Chancellorsville is arguably the best part, with huge numbers of reenactors reliving the deadly assault. It is not to be missed!

Use Your Smartphone on a Battlefield Tour

Why? You can get a top-quality, self-paced tour of a battlefield from respected personalities.

Description: This is one modern development that has no adverse effect on the hallowed ground of Civil War battlefields and will open the door for more people to benefit from the vast knowledge of experienced guides than was ever possible before. Take advantage of your phone's technology to enjoy high-quality tours of major Civil War battlefields from some of the most well-respected historians and personalities in the field. Visit your "app store" or go to www.civilwar.org/battleapp.

Smartphones know where you are and which way you are facing, therefore offering great help when you tour historic places.

Browse Images at the Library of Congress

Why? The Library of Congress offers the best platform and by far the highest resolution available for viewing a vast collection of Civil War photographs and drawings. And it's free.

Description: Go to the Library of Congress website, click "library catalogs," click "prints and photographs," and click either "Civil War Photographs" or "Drawings-Documentary," and have at it. You will gain access to more than 9,000 Civil War images created throughout, and shortly after, the Civil War. You can either browse or search the photographs within each collection. Look at battlefields, soldiers, the living and the dead, scarred landscapes, cities burned and bombed, and every other subject Civil War imagery has to offer.

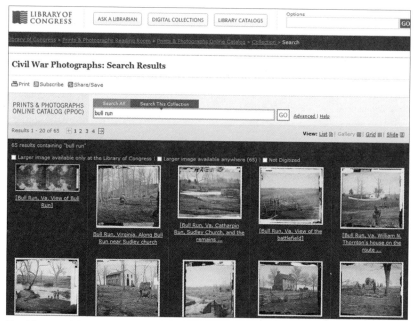

The Library of Congress offers an unparalleled collection and platform to see, download, and use Civil War imagery.

Some of the devastating pictures in this collection, especially those that show dead soldiers on battlefields, shook the North in a way that words could not express. You can view the images on the site or download them to your computer in very, very high resolution—meaning that you can zoom in again and again without the image losing clarity. If you still haven't had enough, check out the online photo collections at the National Archives and the Army Heritage Education Center. Together, these three repositories hold more than 75 percent of all known documentary Civil War photographs.

NATION SPLIT IN TWO

While the American Revolution did in fact create the United States, the Civil War (1861–1865) decided what kind of nation it would become. The Civil War finally resolved two major questions that the Revolution never fully answered: Would the United States be a confederation of sovereign states or an indivisible nation with a powerful national government? And would this nation, born from a belief that all men were created equal, continue to be a slave-holding country?

The Civil War began largely because of significant differences between the free and slave states over whether the national government rightly had the power to keep slavery from spreading to the territories that had yet to become states. When Abraham Lincoln won the presidency in 1860 on the platform to keep slavery out of the remaining territories, seven slave states, beginning with South Carolina, seceded from the Union and formed a new country, the Confederate States of America. The incoming Lincoln administration disputed

the legality of secession and was concerned, among other things, that it would Balkanize the United States.

The Civil War started at Fort Sumter in Charleston Harbor, South Carolina, on April 12, 1861. Trying to claim this United States fort as its own, the Confederate army opened fire on Sumter and eventually forced its surrender. In response, Lincoln called up troops as four more slave states seceded and joined the new Confederacy. By the end of the year, nearly one million armed men were involved in the conflict, which now spanned from fields near Manassas, Virginia, to the mountains of western Virginia to Wilson's Creek, Missouri, Cape Hatteras, North Carolina, and to Port Royal, South Carolina. The fateful year of 1861 saw the bloodiest fighting the young nation had ever experienced, but it proved to be merely a warmup for the horrors to come. The course was set for four years of fighting on a scale so unimaginable that it would claim more American lives than the next century of war combined—the heavy cost of resolving, if not establishing, America's identity.

Union officers at Fort Sumter had become famous even before the shooting started.

STEP INTO 3-D CIVIL WAR PHOTOS

Why? *It is estimated that at least 70 percent of all Civil War documentary photographs were shot as "stereoviews," the 19th century term for today's 3-D. View them in 3-D and you will see them the way the photographers intended.*

Description: Seeing Civil War pictures in 3-D brings them to life. You will be shocked and pleased as the pictures jump right out at you! You'll suddenly understand why Civil War photographers took pictures low to the ground and with odd items in the foreground—to increase the 3-D viewing depth. Visit www.civilwar.org or www.civilwarphotography.org to get started!

Put your glasses on and see Civil War photos as they were meant to be seen!

FIND A CIVIL WAR ANCESTOR

Why? Whether you research your own or somebody else's ancestor, you establish a connection with our forefathers and learn something about the conflict that you otherwise would not have.

Description: Numerous ways exist to research ancestry, many of which are available through your home computer. First you need to find out the soldier's name and unit. Local historical societies usually have genealogical experts who can help with census and other data. Once you have a possible name, the Civil War Soldiers and Sailors System or the website Ancestry.com are very helpful to advance the process. The best online resource is the affordably priced Civil War Research Database. Ultimately, you may wish to visit or engage a researcher, and then ask him to go to the National Archives in Washington, D.C., to secure copies of that soldier's service and pension records. Once you have the specifics, then you can visit the sites where your ancestor fought!

These veterans are looking over their own names on Gettysburg's Pennsylvania Memorial. You can do the same for those long gone.

Climb a Battlefield Observatory

Why? *These platforms give you a bird's-eye view of the field and make it much easier to visualize the disposition of the troops and the progression of a battle.*

Description: Battlefield observation towers offer a fantastic opportunity to take in a beautiful view of the countryside. From your panoramic perch you will be able to see more of the battlefield than the officers of the Federal or Confederate armies could have dreamed! There are observation towers at numerous battlefields, including Gettysburg, Antietam, Chickamauga, and Port Hudson to name only a few, and though these towers were constructed after the battles at these respective fields, they help visitors to comprehend the scope and scale of the fight in a way that is nearly impossible from the ground.

The view from a battlefield observatory is even more rewarding than the climb.

See a Civil War Site Long Gone

Why? The field itself may be gone, but that doesn't mean you can't go and visit the site and honor the event and the people who were there.

Description: Sadly, far too many significant Civil War sites throughout the country have been lost to development. These sites include entire battlefields, prisons, houses, hospitals, and more, all of which held a meaningful connection to the Civil War. Many sites have been paved over and turned into housing developments and shopping centers, among other sad fates. Often there's no way a passing observer could ever know that a piece of Civil War history actually took place there. In fact, locals sometimes seem to go out of their way to make sure of it! Nevertheless, by going to visit these sites and resolving to work for the preservation of other battlefields, we can still remember these places and the people who served and suffered there. This is an altogether fitting way to honor the people who may have died there. Some significant sites that have suffered an unfortunate fate include Seven Pines, Fort Mahone, Libby Prison, Iuka, and, although it's being reclaimed acre by acre, most of the battlefield at Franklin, Tennessee.

The part of Morris Island, South Carolina, that has been reclaimed by the sea includes almost all of the historic Fort Wagner—site of the charge of the 54th Massachusetts.

Visit a Local Civil War Monument

Why? You will not only honor the memory of the soldiers and sailors that died and/or served in the Civil War, but you'll also learn something new.

Description: Numerous cities and towns, especially those east of the Mississippi River, contain monuments to the local soldiers and sailors that

Civil War monuments are all over the United States, including this one in Waltham, Massachusetts.

served in the Civil War. The number and distribution of these monuments is in itself a testament to the commitment that was made by nearly every community over the course of the conflict. Visiting your local monument can be your way of paying homage to the people who sacrificed so much to take part in America's defining struggle. Reading the many names inscribed in stone can be a powerful experience. Go see whose are written there and the deeds they performed so long ago. That's what the monuments were built for!

POINTS WEST
☑ Check off each place as you go!

Points West: Kentucky, Tennessee, Mississippi, and Beyond

*A*lthough more heritage tourists flock to places like Antietam, Gettysburg, and Chickamauga, Civil War sites stretch from Mississippi to Illinois to California. Hidden gems—well preserved and little-visited battlefields like Arkansas' Pea Ridge, Missouri's Wilson's Creek, Louisiana's Port Hudson, New Mexico's Glorieta Pass, and Arizona's Picacho Peak—reward the intrepid traveler, while pivotal battles like Mill Springs and Perryville in Kentucky could have ultimately changed the outcome of the war. Wilson's Creek in Missouri was fought just after the First Battle of Bull Run. Corinth, Mississippi, saw more Civil War soldiers than Gettysburg ever did. Palmito Ranch, Texas, and Picacho Peak, Arizona, claim the last and the farthest west Civil War battles, respectively.

Among the states that saw more fighting in the Civil War, Tennessee and Mississippi have numerous options for enthusiasts. At Shiloh, Tennessee, the bloody fighting ended all hopes for a quick conclusion to the hostilities, while Ulysses S. Grant's exploits at Forts Henry and Donelson earned him a reputation for "Unconditional Surrender." In Mississippi, work continues to permanently protect lesser-known cavalry battlefields such as Tupelo and Brice's Crossroads, while the outstanding Vicksburg National Military Park tells the story of the campaign that split the Confederacy in two.

Spread out these places may be, but they are not only worth the trip, they are essential to a greater understanding of the war.

SEE THE DIVERSE SITES AT MILL SPRINGS
Mill Springs Battlefield, Kentucky

Why? Find out where the Union gained its much needed first major victory of the war.

Description: Although Confederate General Felix K. Zollicoffer's orders were to keep watch over the critical Cumberland Gap, he decided to move west into Kentucky in November 1861. Once in Kentucky, Zollicoffer took up strong defensive positions around Mill Springs. In response, Union General George Thomas was ordered to push his enemy across the Cumberland River and destroy the Confederate forces. Confederate General George Crittenden, Zollicoffer's superior, realizing that Thomas was in the general area, decided that the best course of

The impressive mill at Mill Springs boasts a 40-foot wheel—one of the largest of its kind.

action was to preemptively attack the Federals. Thus, the Confederates attacked General Thomas at Logan's Crossroads in the early morning hours of January 19, 1862.

Initially, the Confederates forced the Union troops to retire, but the Federal army stiffened their resolve and held firm. During the ensuing clash Zollicoffer was himself mortally wounded. In response the Confederates launched a second attack, but were again repulsed. Eventually, Union counterattacks on the Confederate right and left proved successful, forcing the Rebels from the field. Mill Springs decimated Confederate troop strength in eastern Kentucky and opened up a potential invasion route to east Tennessee and perhaps Nashville. Start at the visitors center and be prepared to be impressed with Civil War Kentucky!

Location: 9020 W. Highway 80, Nancy, Kentucky 42544

Visit Kentucky's Largest Battle: Perryville
Perryville Battlefield State Historic Site, Kentucky

Why? This is the site of the largest clash in the Bluegrass state, where the Union army dashed Confederate hopes for control of Kentucky.

Description: Confederate General Braxton Bragg's invasion of Kentucky in the fall of 1862 put Confederate forces on the outskirts of Louisville itself. In response, a Federal army under General Don Carlos Buell, 55,000 strong, advanced to intercept Bragg. Their first meeting occurred when Federal forces skirmished with Confederate cavalry on the Springfield Pike near Perryville as Confederate infantry rushed to the scene. The next morning fighting erupted around Peters Hill as a Union division moved up the pike. Following a brief lull in the action, a Confeder-

The beautiful Perryville Battlefield.

ate division attacked the Union left flank and forced these Federals to fall back.

As Confederate reinforcements arrived, the Federals dug in and made a stubborn stand. Eventually, Union reinforcements arrived on the left flank, stabilized the line, and repulsed the Confederate onslaught. Later in the day Confederate infantry again attacked Union forces on the Springfield Pike. This attack was again repulsed, forcing the Confederates to fall back to Perryville. The Federals gave chase, and skirmishing took place in the streets just before dark. Union reinforcements were now seriously threatening the Confederate left flank, forcing Bragg to withdraw during the night.

After stopping briefly at Harrodsburg, Bragg fled to east Tennessee. The Confederate invasion of Kentucky was over. The Perryville Battlefield is well preserved and interpreted. Start at the visitor center and make sure you check out Open Knob.

Location: 1825 Battlefield Rd., Perryville, Kentucky 40468

Find Familiar Names at Lexington Cemetery
Lexington, Kentucky

Why? *The cemetery is an eerie final resting place for many of Kentucky's most famous sons and daughters.*

Description: Alongside the bronze marker that commemorates the arrival of Europeans in Lexington stands the gateway to the city's storied graveyard. Visitors to this famed cemetery will find the gravesites of many of Lexington's most prominent Civil War– and antebellum-era figures, including Confederate General John Hunt Morgan, John C. Breckinridge, Henry Brainerd McClellan, U.S. Representative Henry Clay, relatives of Mary Todd Lincoln, and many enlisted Union and Confederate soldiers. The cemetery is also home to two large monuments dedicated to the Union and Confederate dead of Lexington. Visitors are encouraged to pick up a self-guided walking tour, which highlights both natural and historical points of interest.

Location: 833 West Main St., Lexington, Kentucky 40508

SEE A CAMP YOU NEVER KNEW: CAMP NELSON
Nicholasville, Kentucky

Why? *Camp Nelson was the site of a major supply and recruiting station for the Union army throughout the Civil War.*

Description: Camp Nelson was a very important supply depot for the Army of of the Ohio and the Army of the Cumberland. Camp Nelson supplied the Union invasion of Knoxville and the Battles of Saltville in southwest Virginia. It also grew to become the third largest recruiting base for African American soldiers in the United States, with 10,000 black soldiers recruited here. More than 400 acres of the original 4,000-acre campsite are preserved for interpretation. The only surviving building (the officers' quarters) of the 300 at the camp has been restored and is open for visitors. A three-mile trail will take you through the depot section and the northern line of fortifications.

Location: 6612 Danville Rd., Nicholasville, Kentucky 40356

Monument at Camp Nelson.

See Where Grant Became Famous: Fort Donelson
Fort Donelson National Battlefield, Tennessee

Why? Find out how Ulysses S. Grant earned the moniker of "Unconditional Surrender" Grant and how he gained the admiration of a nation desperate for heroes.

Description: In an effort to secure Middle Tennessee for the Union, General Ulysses S. Grant moved his army toward Fort Donelson in early February. On February 14, Navy gunboats under Flag Officer Andrew H. Foote opened fire on Donelson but were forced to retire as a result of sustaining too much damage from Donelson's water batteries. The next day, after their fort had been surrounded by Grant's men, the Confederates, led by General John B. Floyd, launched a surprise attack against Grant's army, hoping to open up a pathway for escape. Grant was quickly able to rally his men, however, and launch a counterattack of his own.

The Fort Donelson National Battlefield.

Ultimately, Floyd lost his nerve and ordered his Confederates back to their entrenchments, ultimately sealing their fate. On the morning of February 16, Floyd and his second-in-command, Brig. Gen. Gideon J. Pillow, turned their commands over to General Simon Bolivar Buckner, who agreed to unconditional surrender terms with Grant. In the process, more than 14,000 Confederate soldiers were captured, guaranteeing Federal control of the Cumberland River, the City of Nashville, and most of Middle Tennessee. The victory also ensured the rapid rise of an obscure but dogged general—Ulysses S. Grant.

Location: Donelson Parkway and Ft. Donelson Park Road, Dover, Tennessee 37058

FIGHTING THE CIVIL WAR

The basic infantry unit was the regiment, intended to be one thousand officers and men at full strength. Regiments were raised geographically and designated with a number and their state of origin. Two or more regiments were grouped together to form a brigade, often fighting in concert and forging a strong unit identity such as the Stonewall Brigade, the Irish Brigade, or the Iron Brigade. Two or more brigades formed a division; divisions grouped into corps and corps into armies.

In Civil War tactics—whether offensive or defensive—the main combat arm of any army was the infantry, most often deployed for combat in a long "line of battle," two ranks deep. Tacticians aimed to have soldiers function in a coordinated manner, achieving maximum force and avoiding the danger of being destroyed "in detail," unit by unit. Battle lines delivered the most effective firepower, but offensive firepower alone could not guarantee success. Attackers

Infantry at drill.

had to charge against defensive positions usually manned in lines of battle and often fortified with field works, especially later in the war. Ideally, aggressors preferred to "roll up" enemy battle lines lengthwise with a flank attack. To counter this threat, defensive tacticians sought opportunities to anchor their lines on impassable barriers such as rivers or mountains, or by "refusing" a portion of the line at a right angle to the main body. Throughout the war, both armies used open-order (typically a strung-out, irregular single line) deployment to cover their front and flanks with skirmishers who screened the main body of troops.

An explosion of new military technology shaped Civil War tactics, particularly the advent of the rifled firearms. More powerful and with greater accuracy over a longer distance, rifled muskets were far more deadly than their smoothbore musket predecessor that had been standard issue as recently as the Mexican War. As both sides learned how best to employ their new firearms, infantry began to regularly "dig in" when adopting a defensive stance by assembling earthworks—clear forerunners to the trench warfare of World

Artillery in the field.

War I. Still, infantry attacks continued to produce heavy casualties due to outdated tactical formations.

Terrain and technology conspired to greatly change the traditional roles of Civil War artillery and cavalry. Cannons came in all shapes and sizes and could concentrate fire upon targets near and far, large and small—enemy artillery, bodies of troops, buildings, vessels, and more. Cavalry were the army's chief scouts, providing tactical intelligence for the larger force. By the middle of the war, moreover, cavalry units were using their mobility to reach key spots on the battlefield quickly, dismount, and fight on foot with their breech-loading carbines. It was rare for cavalry to fight with saber and pistol, and even rarer for them to engage in mounted pursuits of defeated enemies.

Cavalry generals George Custer and Alfred Pleasonton.

TOUR THE PRISTINE NATIONAL MILITARY PARK: SHILOH
Shiloh National Battlefield, Tennessee

Why? Learn about the Civil War where it still feels like 1862: SHILOH!

Description: On April 6–7, 1862, Confederate forces under Generals Albert Sidney Johnston and P. G. T. Beauregard launched a major, surprise attack against General Ulysses S. Grant's Army of the Tennessee. Initially, the Confederate attack was a great success. However, the Confederate battle lines soon became confused as Grant's men fell back in the direction of Pittsburg Landing on the Tennessee River. General Johnston was killed during the first day of the battle, and Beauregard, upon taking command, decided against attacking the final Union position that night, instead opting to regroup and prepare for the next day. Union General Don Carlos Buell's Army of the Ohio arrived during the night and ultimately turned the tide of the battle when he and Grant

Few battlefields can boast such remarkable opportunities as Shiloh for seeing what the soldiers saw.

launched a massive counterattack along the entire line the next morning. As a result, the Confederates were forced to retreat.

Union casualties numbered 13,047, while the Confederates suffered 10,699. The two-day total of 23,746 casualties amounted to more than America suffered in the American Revolution, the War of 1812, and the Mexican-American War combined. Both sides were appalled with the carnage. Yet, at the time, no one suspected that this, sadly, was only the beginning. Far bigger and bloodier battles were only a short march down the road. Today, visitors have the opportunity to tour this beautifully preserved battlefield to learn how men of North and South met in battle in a place of supposed peace: *Shiloh*.

Location: 1055 Pittsburg Landing Rd., Shiloh, Tennessee 38376

Stand Where General Albert Sidney Johnston Died
Shiloh National Military Park, Tennessee

Why? Visit the place where General Johnston lost his life and where the Confederacy was forced to come to terms with the loss of its highest ranking general in the field.

Description: During the afternoon of the first day of the Battle of Shiloh, while the Confederate Army attempted to turn Grant's left flank and seize Pittsburg Landing, Commanding General Albert Sidney Johnston was struck by a stray Minie ball below his right knee. The bullet ripped through Johnston's knee, tearing a vital artery and causing severe and ultimately mortal bleeding. Tennessee Governor Isham G. Harris, who was serving as a volunteer aide, came upon Johnston reeling in the saddle, and led him down to the protected ravine where Johnston died only a few minutes later. Today, a historic tree trunk stands at the site where the oak tree stood under which Johnston received his fatal wound. There is some dispute, however, as to whether the event happened there or at another nearby location.

Location: Shiloh National Military Park, 1055 Pittsburg Landing, Shiloh, Tennessee 38376

Monument at or near the site of Albert Sidney Johnston's death.

STAND ON CARNTON'S PORCH
Franklin, Tennessee

Why? *Carnton and the surrounding plantation grounds saw some of the Civil War's bloodiest hours of fighting during the Battle of Franklin.*

Description: Had you been standing here on November 30, 1864, you would have been watching wave after wave of Confederates on their way to attacking the well-entrenched Federal lines in a terrible and devastating battle. Because Carnton is less than one mile from the front, you would have been able to see the fire, smoke, and explosions from the battlefield. After the battle, Carnton became a hospital for more than 6,000 wounded Confederates.

On the back porch, four Confederate generals' bodies—Patrick Cleburne, John Adams, Otho F. Strahl, and Hiram B. Granbury—were laid to rest a few hours after the battle. Hundreds of the Confederate wounded were aided by Carrie McGavock and her family. Some claim that there were as many as 300 Confederate men cared for by the McGavocks inside Carnton alone. In the process, the floors became permanently stained with blood. Today, the McGavocks' sacrifice is remembered in the adjoining McGavock Confederate Cemetery. The book *The Widow of the South* is based upon the life of Carrie McGavock.

Location: 1345 Carnton Lane, Franklin, Tennessee 37064

The house, grounds, exhibits, and blood-stained interior make Carnton a key place to visit.

SEE BULLET-RIDDLED HISTORY AT THE CARTER HOUSE
Franklin, Tennessee

Why? *Visit the home and its simple outbuildings that mark the ground upon which the Battle of Franklin reached its bloody conclusion.*

Description: Built in 1830 by Fountain Branch Carter, the Carter House sits at the epicenter of the battle of Franklin. Before the battle, the house served as a Union command post, forcing the Carter family to take refuge in the cellar throughout the infamous battle. After the battle, the house was used as a hospital.

Today, the house and grounds, encompassing some ten acres, have been preserved. This registered National Historic Landmark is open to the public and serves as a fitting memorial to the Carter Family and the men who endured the Battle of Franklin. Visitors come face to face with the evidence of some one thousand extant bullet holes in the structures. Ultimately, the Battle of Franklin proved a key turning point in what turned out to be a decisive campaign. Learn about that decisive campaign and the bloody conclusion of Hood's Middle Tennessee Campaign where the battle raged the fiercest—the Carter House.

Location: 1140 Columbia Ave., Franklin, Tennessee 37064

From bullet holes to the tragic family story, the Carter house is unforgettable.

Learn How Chattanooga Was Defended
Chattanooga, Tennessee, and area

Why? From the panoramic views atop Lookout Mountain to the rugged terrain of Missionary Ridge, this is a battlefield that must be studied in person.

Description: Though geographically dispersed, the Chickamauga & Chattanooga National Military Park preserves an impressive array of sites that tells the story of the battles for control of this junction in November of 1863. After the November 23 capture of Orchard Knob, Union General Grant had a perfect observation post for the grand fighting that followed. On November 24, Union General Joseph Hooker's forces won the Battle of Lookout Mountain. Looking up at the mountain, you'll wonder how such an impressive height could ever be carried. Standing on a plateau at the Craven House, you'll see why defending the crest and the ground below it required a lot of soldiers—more men than Confederate General Braxton Bragg had or was willing to dedicate. Point Park, atop the crest of Lookout Mountain, is one of the most popular features in the area. The Visitor Center also features James Walker's 13 x 30-foot painting entitled "The Battle of Lookout Mountain."

Only by seeing Lookout Mountain in person, looming above the city, can you grasp Grant's daunting task in the fall of 1863.

On November 25, Union General Grant and Union General George Thomas watched in amazement from Orchard Knob as Federal soldiers—without orders—charged up Missionary Ridge and captured the seemingly impregnable position. Missionary Ridge, a 400-foot high, 20-mile-long mountain barrier, runs east of the city of Chattanooga. The fall of Missionary Ridge, along with the Confederate defeat at Lookout Mountain, ended the Confederate control of Chattanooga and its vital rail junction. Grant arrived in October to find a besieged, starving army, and in less than two months he had opened supply lines, lifted the siege, and knocked Bragg back into Georgia.

Though today only glimpses of the Missionary Ridge Battlefield are still visible, there are small National Park Service areas, known as "reservations," located along Crest Road with monuments and interpretive markers.

Location: Orchard Knob: East Fifth Street and North Orchard Knob Avenue, Chattanooga, Tennessee 37404

Lookout Mountain: Point Lookout Visitor Center, 1110 East Brow Rd., Lookout Mountain, Tennessee 37350

Missionary Ridge: US 27 and South Crest Road, Rossville, Georgia 30741

Looking from Orchard Knob to Missionary Ridge.

THE CASUALTIES

More than 3.2 million soldiers served in the American Civil War, and approximately 620,000 of those perished—more than the total American death toll for the Revolutionary War, War of 1812, Mexican-American War, Spanish-American War, World War I, World War II, and the Korean War combined. The Battle of Shiloh alone produced more combat deaths than all American wars fought up to that point.

When discussing Civil War casualties, one of the most common misconceptions is that the term "casualty" is synonymous with death. Casualty figures actually include the dead (fatalities, killed-in-action, and mortally wounded), wounded, and missing or captured. In a typical battle, fewer than 20 percent of those listed as casualties would have been killed. An estimated one in seven wounded soldiers, however, later died of wounds. All told, historians estimate that more than two-thirds of the 620,000 men who perished during the Civil War died as a result of disease and not from battle.

Incomplete, inaccurate, and destroyed records, coupled with the frequent use of the nebulous term "missing in action," make it impossible to determine precise casualty figures, especially in the Confederacy.

Dead Confederate soldiers near Spotsylvania.

	TOTAL	UNION	CONFEDERATE
Served	3,211,067	2,128,948	1,082,119
Casualties	1,086,979	596,670	490,309
Killed and Mortally Wounded	204,070	110,070	94,000
Wounded	469,226	275,200	194,026
Missing and Captured	413,683	211,400	202,283
Died of Disease	416,152	250,152	166,000
Killed and Died of Disease	620,222	360,222	260,000

A hospital in Washington, D.C.

Confederate prisoners in Virginia's "Punch Bowl."

Where Union prisoners were held at Belle Isle.

SEE THE SITE WITH THE HIGHEST CASUALTY RATE— STONES RIVER

Stones River Battlefield, Tennessee

Why? *Visit the site of one of the war's rare winter battles, where the Union gained an important New Year's victory . . . sort of.*

Description: On the morning of December 31, 1862, General Braxton Bragg and his 37,000-man Confederate Army of Tennessee attacked the Federal right flank of General William S. Rosecrans' 44,000-man Union Army of the Cumberland. The Confederates initially pushed the Union line back to the Nashville Pike, but from then on the Union line held firm. Federal reinforcements arrived late in the afternoon to stiffen their resolve, and before the fighting concluded, the Federals had created a

Impressive rock formations mingle with horrible struggle at the Slaughter Pen.

new, stronger line. On January 1, both armies simply marked time. Bragg determined that Rosecrans would withdraw, but the next morning still found him in position.

During the late afternoon hours, Bragg sent a division to attack a Union division that had crossed Stones River and had formed a strong defensive position on the bluff east of the river. The Confederates drove the majority of the Federals back across McFadden Ford, but with the help of artillery, the Federals stopped the attack, forcing the Confederates to withdraw back to their original positions. Bragg withdrew from the field on January 4, 1863, and retreated to Tullahoma, Tennessee. Rosecrans opted not to give chase, but as the Confederates left, he claimed the victory. Stones River, called Murfreesboro by the Confederates, helped boost Northern morale as Southern advances had now been pushed back in the East, West, and Trans-Mississippi.

Location: 3501 Old Nashville Hwy., Murfreesboro, Tennessee 37129

Visit Corinth: Besieged, Secured, and Defended
Corinth, Mississippi

Why? *When Confederate General P. G. T. Beauregard retreated from Shiloh, he fell back to this important rail junction. Learn why it took the Union so long to reach this railroad town.*

Description: The "Cross City" of Corinth, Mississippi, sat at the crossover junction of the Memphis & Charleston and the Mobile & Ohio Railroads. Located in the northeast corner of the state near the Tennessee border, Corinth is only twenty-two miles from Shiloh Battlefield. Confederate forces retreated to this important logistical junction following that harrowing clash in April 1862—where they waited ever patiently for the

The only photos showing dead on a western Civil War battlefield were taken at Battery Robinett, Corinth.

Union advance. The advance under the cautious General Henry Halleck was slow. Union troops dug in along the way, at every step.

By the time Halleck's siege was laid, the Confederates had left in good order. Later that year, Confederate forces tried to recapture the city but were turned back at the Battle of Corinth (also known as the Second Battle of Corinth). The fighting was particularly fierce at Battery Robinett, and a photographer managed to capture the dead on the field soon after. Today, visitors can tour Battery Robinett, a reconstruction of one of seven batteries built by the Union army after the siege of Corinth in the spring of 1862. This prominent earthen defense stood at the center of the Union line in this second battle of Corinth in the fall of 1862, making it the most famous spot on the battlefield today. Make sure you visit the impressive Corinth Civil War Interpretive Center. See its acclaimed video, pick up maps for the self-guided walking and driving tours, and see the exhibits that cover not only Corinth but other aspects of the war.

Location: 501 West Linden St., Corinth, Mississippi 38834

LEARN OF FORREST'S WIZARDRY AT BRICE'S CROSSROADS
Brice's Crossroads National Battlefield Site, Mississippi

Why? *Visit the battlefield where General Nathan Bedford Forrest cemented his reputation as the "Wizard of the Saddle."*

Description: In June of 1864, General Nathan Bedford Forrest set out to destroy the Nashville & Chattanooga Railroad, a crucial line of supply for General William T. Sherman's Union army in Georgia. On June 10, 1864, at 9:30 a.m., one half mile east of Brice's Crossroads, Federal cavalry under Union General Samuel Sturgis ran into the Confederate Kentucky Brigade and the battle began in earnest. By 11 a.m. Forrest was pushing the Federals back toward the crossroads as the Federal infantry arrived. By 5 p.m., after enveloping both of the Federal flanks and launching an

En route from the visitor center to the actual crossroads, interpretive signage will guide you.

audacious frontal attack, Forrest had completely destroyed Sturgis' line, which forced the Federals to retreat.

An overturned wagon at the Tishomingo Creek Bridge delayed the retreat and allowed Forrest to capture sixteen artillery pieces, and several arms and ammunition-filled supply wagons. Through the efforts of a brigade of United States Colored Troops executing a series of defensive actions, most of Sturgis' army avoided capture. After the battle Sturgis was demoted and exiled to the far West. For Forrest, this brilliant tactical victory against a superior opponent cemented his reputation as one of the greatest mounted infantry leaders of the war. Much of the battlefield remains in an excellent state of preservation. Start your visit at the nearby visitor center.

Location: Route 370 and County Road 6380, Guntown, Mississippi 38849

See the Smallest National Civil War Park: Tupelo
Tupelo, Mississippi

Why? *Find out how Union infantry saved Sherman's supply lines from the legendary Confederate cavalier, Nathan Bedford Forrest.*

Description: Though consisting of only a single preserved acre, this park protects the site of an important battle that prevented a distracted Confederate General Nathan Bedford Forrest from disrupting Sherman's supply lines during the Atlanta Campaign of 1864. The July 14–15 battle involved more than 20,000 soldiers and consisted of a series of Confederate attacks that were repulsed with heavy losses. Despite his success in repelling attacks, Union General Andrew Smith grew increasingly concerned about his supplies and ordered a retreat. While the Federal command moved northward, Confederate forces attacked Smith's men again. The Federals formed a line, pushed the Confederates off the ridge and forced them to retreat. Although there was no clear-cut winner, the Federal forces had accomplished the goal of keeping Forrest far from rail lines in Tennessee. This was the last engagement between General Forrest and Union infantry.

Location: West Main Street and Monument Drive, Tupelo, Mississippi 38801

THE FIRST, THE MOST, AND THE FARTHEST

The American Civil War began on April 12, 1861, and ended in the spring of 1865 with the surrender of Confederate armies. It involved more than three million American soldiers on both sides, and total deaths reached a staggering 620,000. In financial terms, the war cost the U.S. government $2.5 million daily, according to a January 1863 estimate. A final tally done in 1879 placed the total cost at $6.19 billion for the Union, with another nearly $2.1 billion spent by the Confederacy. By 1906, pensions and other benefits for Northern veterans had cost the government another $3.3 billion—a figure far greater than the war's original cost.

The first engagement of the Civil War took place on April 12, 1861, when Confederates in Charleston, South Carolina, fired on the Federal garrison at Fort Sumter. The first land battle of the war took place at Big Bethel in Newport News, Virginia, on June 10, 1861, followed in the coming months by First Manassas and Wilson's Creek. The last significant battle of the Civil War was at Palmito Ranch, Texas, May 12 and 13, 1865.

Although not every state saw a battle within its borders, each state was affected by the Civil War in some way. Every state and territory sent its human

The U.S. Treasury Department.

treasure off to fight, and many had prisoner of war camps and hospitals. But battles did occur in unexpected spaces. The Civil War's northernmost fight took place at St. Albans, Vermont, during an October 19, 1864, raid, while its westernmost battle took place at Picacho Peak, Arizona, on April 15, 1862. Alcatraz Island off of San Francisco, California, served as a Civil War prison.

The Civil War also saw a variety of "firsts" that affected warfare, healthcare, and politics forever. Military firsts included: workable machine guns, ironclad warships, successful submarines, soldier conscription, aerial reconnaissance, anti-aircraft fire, electrically exploded bombs and torpedoes, fixed ammunition, field trenches, land-mines, readily available long-range rifles, the Congressional Medal of Honor, military use of the telegraph and railroad, naval torpedoes, railroad artillery, repeating rifles, revolving gun turrets, the periscope, telescopic sights for rifles, and wire entanglements. Healthcare firsts included an organized corps for Army ambulances, surgeons, and nurses; hospital ships; wide-scale use of anesthetics for the wounded; and a burgeoning understanding of germs and how they brought in diseases. Finally, long-lasting political firsts from the Civil War include the income tax, cigarette tax, tobacco tax, and legal voting rights for servicemen.

Among other things, the former Customs House in Richmond served as the Treasury of the Confederacy.

VISIT THE CITADEL CITY: VICKSBURG
Vicksburg National Military Park, Mississippi

Why? *Control of the mighty Mississippi River rested in the fate of this Citadel City. Find out why July 4 is remembered for something other than America's birthday in this southern river town.*

Description: The 1,800-acre Vicksburg National Military Park commemorates the campaign and siege of Vicksburg, waged from May 18 to July 4, 1863. The city of Vicksburg fell to Union General Ulysses S. Grant on July 4, 1863, after a forty-seven-day siege that included extensive land and

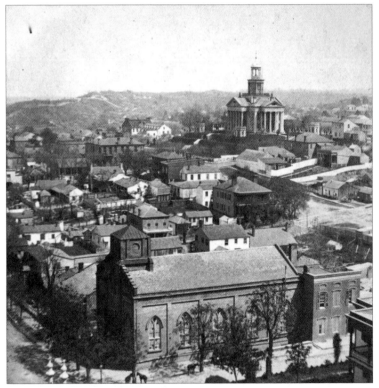

Vicksburg, Mississippi, in the 19th century.

naval operations. The fall of Vicksburg along with the victory at nearby Port Hudson gave the Union complete control of the Mississippi River, destroyed a major Confederate supply line that ran east-west through Vicksburg, and effectively cut the Confederacy in two.

The park contains 1,325 monuments and markers, more than twenty miles of the original trenches and earthworks, a sixteen-mile tour road, a 12.5-mile walking trail, two antebellum homes including the historic Shirley house, 144 cannons, the restored Union ironclad gunboat USS *Cairo* (which sank on December 12, 1862, on the Yazoo River, and was recovered in 1964), Grant's Canal site where the Union army tried to build a canal in an attempt to allow its ships to bypass Confederate artillery fire, and Vicksburg National Cemetery. The *Cairo*, which is also known as the "Hardluck Ironclad," was the first U.S. ship ever to be sunk by either a torpedo or a mine.

Location: 3201 Clay St., Vicksburg, Mississippi 39183

The Shirley House is a key stop on any Vicksburg tour.

WALK THROUGH THE USS *CAIRO* SKELETON
Vicksburg National Military Park, Mississippi

Why? Stand on the deck of a gunboat that sat at the bottom of the Yazoo River for more than a century before a team of National Park Service historians raised her to the surface.

Description: On the morning of December 12, 1862, disaster struck the USS *Cairo.* While on routine patrol, the gunboat was rocked by two massive torpedo explosions and sank twelve minutes later (without any loss of life), giving the ship the dubious distinction of being the first in history to be sunk by an electrically detonated torpedo. More than one hundred years later, in 1965, the USS *Cairo* was raised from the murky waters. Her armor was carefully removed, cleaned, and stored. The two massive engines were disassembled, cleaned, and put back together. The hull was braced internally to prevent collapse, and a sprinkler system was installed to help keep the white oak timbers from warping. Today, the ironclad and a treasure trove of artifacts recovered from the ship are on display at the USS *Cairo* Museum in Vicksburg National Military Park.

Location: 3201 Clay St., Vicksburg, Mississippi 39183

The National Park Service has created a dedicated interpretive center around this one-of-a-kind relic of the war.

"Full Speed Ahead" to Mobile Bay
Fort Morgan, Alabama

Why? *Learn about an important sea battle and the place where the famous phrase "Damn the torpedoes—full speed ahead!" made its debut.*

Description: On August 5, 1864, Admiral David G. Farragut launched a major assault on the Confederate fleet operating in Mobile Bay as well as Fort Gaines, Fort Morgan, and other Confederate positions that guarded the entrance to the bay itself. In the ensuing naval battle, known to history as the Battle of Mobile Bay, Farragut made a seemingly rash but successful run through a minefield that allowed his fleet to get beyond the range of the shore-based guns. To the remonstrations of others, he said, "Damn the torpedoes—full speed ahead!" Once Farragut cleared these guns, his fleet quickly reduced the Confederate fleet down to a single vessel, the ironclad CSS *Tennessee*. Amazingly, instead of retiring, the *Tennessee* engaged the entire Federal fleet until her armor proved useless and she was finally forced to retreat. Once the *Tennessee* surrendered, the three forts guarding the bay surrendered within the next few days, leaving Union forces with complete control of the lower Mobile Bay—the last major port on the Gulf of Mexico east of the Mississippi River still under Confederate control. With Mobile Bay in Federal hands, the Union blockade of this region was officially complete.

Location: Western terminus of AL 180, Gasque, Alabama 36542

Fort Gaines, Alabama.

See the Last Bastion on the Mississippi: Port Hudson
Port Hudson State Historic Site, Louisiana

Why? *Visit the site of one of the longest sieges in United States military history, where black Union soldiers fought for one of the first times.*

Description: Aiding General Ulysses S. Grant's offensive against Vicksburg, Union General Nathaniel P. Banks' army advanced against the Confederates at Port Hudson on the Mississippi. On May 27, after his initial frontal assaults were repulsed, Banks settled into a siege that lasted forty-eight days. Banks attempted another assault on June 14 and was repulsed yet again by the Confederates. On July 9, 1863, after hearing of the fall of Vicksburg, the Confederate garrison at Port Hudson believed there was now no hope and finally surrendered. This opened the Mississippi River to Federal navigation all the way to New Orleans and ensured a steady flow of supplies to Union armies operating in the Deep South.

Location: 236 Highway 61, Jackson, Louisiana 70748

Port Hudson during the Civil War.

Tour Pea Ridge National Military Park
Pea Ridge Battlefield, Arkansas

Why? *Though outnumbered by the Confederate army, Union perseverance at Pea Ridge all but guaranteed Federal control of Missouri for the remainder of the war.*

Description: On March 6–8, 1862, the 10,500-man Union Army of the Southwest and the 16,200-man Confederate Army of the West squared off in two different engagements, one at Leetown and the other at Elkhorn Tavern, on the plain known as Pea Ridge. On the night of March 6, Confederate General Earl Van Dorn attempted to outflank the Union position near Pea Ridge, splitting his army into two columns.

Learning of Van Dorn's advance, the Federals moved north. This Federal response, coupled with the death of two Confederate generals,

Pea Ridge, or Elkhorn Tavern, Arkansas.

General Ben McCulloch and General James McQueen McIntosh, halted the Confederate attack at Leetown. Meanwhile, Van Dorn led a second column to meet the Federals at Elkhorn Tavern. The following day, General Samuel R. Curtis launched a counterattack near the Elkhorn Tavern that slowly pushed the Confederates back. Running low on ammunition, Van Dorn left the battlefield. This important Union victory guaranteed that Missouri would remain under Union control, and it paved the way for the commencement of Ulysses S. Grant's legendary Vicksburg campaign.

Location: 15930 Highway 62 East, Garfield, Arkansas 72732

See Abraham Lincoln's Springfield Home
Springfield, Illinois

Why? *Visit the only home Abraham Lincoln owned.*

Description: Built in 1839, this house was bought by Lincoln and his wife, Mary Todd Lincoln, in 1844. It was the only home that Lincoln ever owned. Restored to its 1860 appearance and situated at the corner of Eighth and Jackson Streets, the twelve-room, Greek revival house belonged to the Lincolns for seventeen years. During the time he lived there, Lincoln was elected to the House of Representatives in 1846 and elected president in 1860. The National Park Service ranger-led tours of the house focus on these seventeen years, beginning with Lincoln's rise as a successful lawyer, stretching to his entry into politics, and culminating in his successful presidential campaign. Along with Lincoln's home, many other structures in the four-block area have also been preserved. Two related houses in this historic district are also open to visitors.

Location: 426 South 7th St., Springfield, Illinois 62703

Lincoln's home sits amidst a larger, well-preserved 19th-century street scene.

TOUR THE BULL RUN OF THE WEST: WILSON'S CREEK
Wilson's Creek National Battlefield, Missouri

Why? This is the site of the first major battle west of the Mississippi River, and the place where the first Union general was killed in combat.

Description: General Nathaniel Lyon's Army of the West was at Springfield, Missouri, as Confederate troops led by General Ben McCulloch approached. At around 5 a.m. on August 10, 1861, Lyon and Colonel Franz Sigel attacked the Confederates at Wilson's Creek. Confederate cavalry was forced back from Bloody Hill. Confederates launched three separate assaults but each time they failed to break through the Federal lines. Lyon was killed during this battle and was replaced by General Samuel D. Sturgis.

Wilson's Creek, Missouri.

During the confusion over command, the Confederates routed Sigel's column south of Skegg's Branch, but after the Confederates made their third attack, which concluded around 11 a.m., they began to withdraw. The Yankees, however, were tired and running low on ammunition. Thus, General Sturgis ordered a retreat back to Springfield, Missouri. The Confederates were in no shape to pursue but could claim a victory. Five Medals of Honor were awarded to Union soldiers who fought in the battle. Today, the battlefield, sometimes called "The Bull Run of the West," has changed very little, and even though preservation efforts did not begin until the 1950s, it looks much as it did in 1861.

Location: 6424 West Farm Rd. 182, Republic, Missouri 65738

SEE THE FINAL BATTLEFIELD: PALMITO RANCH
Brownsville, Texas

Why? Fort Sumter may get all the glory as the first clash—but Palmito was truly the last.

Description: Well over a month after Lee had surrendered to Grant at Appomattox, the Battle of Palmito Ranch pitted the Confederacy's hard-fighting Trans-Mississippi Department against its battle-hardened Federal adversaries one last time. Marking the final attempt by Federal forces to gain control of the Lower Rio Grande region, the Battle of Palmito Ranch raged from May 12 to 13, 1865. Ultimately, this final Confederate attempt to protect their clandestine cotton-shipping operations would be remembered as the last legitimate clash of the four-year conflict.

Location: Palmito Hill Road, Brownsville, Texas 78521

Visit New Mexico's Glorieta Pass
Pecos National Historical Park, New Mexico

Why? This is where the West was won . . . by the Union!

Description: At Pecos National Historical Park visitors have the opportunity to visit several significant Civil War sites: the Glorieta Pass battlefield, Apache Canyon, and Pigeon's Branch. Fought over a series of days in late March, 1862, these battles dashed any hope for Confederate victory in the far West and ended the Confederate attempt to seize supplies at Fort Union. These relatively small clashes ultimately sealed the fate of the West and saved both Colorado and California from falling under rebel control. The park also maintains Kozlowski's Ranch, which served as a Union headquarters.

Location: Pecos National Historical Park, two miles south of Pecos on Highway 63, Pecos, New Mexico 87552

Glorieta Pass, New Mexico.

Visit the Westernmost Battlefield: Picacho Peak
Picacho, Arizona

Why? Go West . . . all the way to the westernmost of Civil War clashes and find out about this overlooked western rebel victory.

Description: In February of 1862, a group of Confederate Rangers under the command of Captain Sherod Hunter raised the Confederate flag in Tucson, Arizona, as part of an attempt to create an ocean-to-ocean Confederacy. In response, a Union "Column from California" under the command of James H. Carelton set out in pursuit. On April 15, 1862, Union cavalry from this California detachment under Lieutenant James Barrett met with these Confederates near Picacho Peak. During the battle that followed, Barrett was killed almost immediately and combat ensued for more than ninety minutes before the Federals retreated. Although this Confederate victory may have delayed Federal forces, only one month later the Californians took Tucson without firing a shot.

Location: Picacho Peak Road, Picacho, Arizona 85141

Picacho Peak. Photo by Aznebuelae33

EXPLORE THE DRUM BARRACKS CIVIL WAR MUSEUM
Wilmington, California

Why? *The Drum Barracks played a pivotal role for the Union cause and is the sole Civil War-era military facility in the Los Angeles area.*

Description: While major Civil War battles raged in the East, soldiers from California helped to keep California in the Union and repel Confederates from the territories of Arizona and New Mexico. The Drum Barracks, named after General Richard Coulter Drum, was the main staging, training, and supply base for area military operations. Camp Drum was the home of the California Column, formed and then commanded by Colonel James Henry Carleton. In 1862, Texas Volunteers had seized control of the Arizona and New Mexico territories for the Confederacy. From Drum Barracks, Colonel Carleton led some 2,350 men on a march to Santa Fe. En route, part of the California Column took part in the Battle of Picacho Pass, which proved to be the Civil War's westernmost engagement in which soldiers suffered casualties. Today, the Drum Barracks Civil War Museum is located in the last remaining wooden building of Drum Barracks.

Location: 1052 Banning Blvd., Wilmington, California 90744

The Drum Barracks.

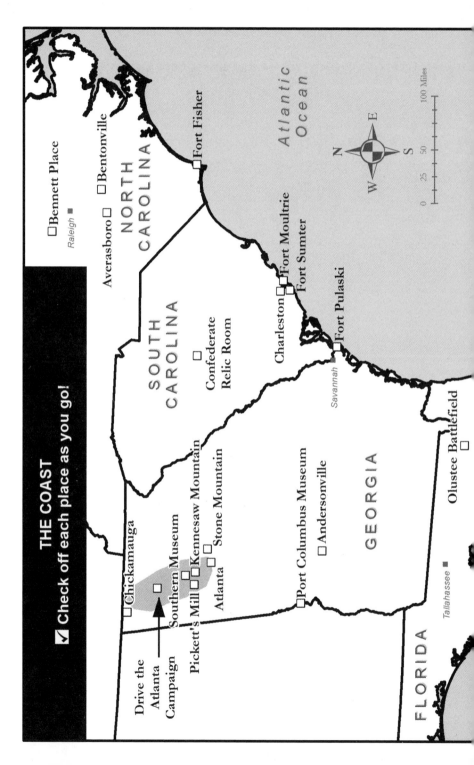

THE COAST: GEORGIA, THE CAROLINAS, AND FLORIDA

The beautiful coastal region offers much for the Civil War adventurer. From battlefields to forts to museums, there is plenty to see and do to enrich your understanding of many aspects of Civil War history.

The strategic importance of ports and waterways led to a tenacious defense of such resources. Many coastal sites were significant until the very close of the war. When you visit Charleston, South Carolina, you can see where the first shots of the Civil War were fired at Fort Sumter, as well as explore other fortifications of war—in the city, in Charleston Harbor, on nearby islands, and spanning the coast from Fort Fisher in North Carolina to Fort Pulaski in Savannah, Georgia. See remains of the Confederate submarine HL *Hunley*, which changed naval warfare forever during its final, fatal mission in 1864. Go to Andersonville, Georgia, site of the war's most notorious prisoner of war camp, which illustrates the horrors experienced by individual soldiers.

Numerous museums across the region help you learn about particular aspects of the Civil War, like railroads and firearms, in great depth. Major battlefields Chickamauga, Kennesaw Mountain, Pickett's Mill, and Bentonville help you learn how the last half of the war unfolded and how the character of these fights in "the west" were different from those in the east. In North Carolina, you can see how all this fighting ended up at the Bennett Place, site of the Civil War's largest surrender of Confederate troops.

SEE AN ARRAY OF SMALL ARMS AT CHICKAMAUGA
Chickamauga and Chattanooga National Military Park, Georgia

Why? *In addition to its incredible gun collection, the Chickamauga Visitor Center fosters broad education about the battle and surrounding campaigns.*

Description: The first stop at Chickamauga should be at the Battlefield Visitor Center, which boasts a topographical electronic map that provides a good visual overview of the fight, a film that explains the events leading up to it, and numerous exhibits and maps designed to get you excited to go out and tour the battlefield. The center also contains the impressive Fuller Gun Collection, with more than 300 different types of small arms on display. Narrated, self-guided auto tours with maps are available to take you to all the major spots on the Chickamauga National Battlefield.

Location: 3370 Lafayette Rd., Fort Oglethorpe, Georgia 30742

SEE WHERE GEORGE THOMAS BECAME THE ROCK
Chickamauga and Chattanooga National Military Park, Georgia

Why? *Chickamauga was the bloodiest battle of the west and the second largest of the war. Seeing this impressive battlefield, especially the Brotherton Farm and Snodgrass Hill, is essential to understanding the war in the west.*

Description: Civil War troops savagely fought the Battle of Chickamauga over several thousand acres of wooded land. These troops, under Union General Rosecrans and Confederate General Bragg, were all but evenly matched. But by September 20, the second or third day of the battle depending on how you count it, thousands of Confederates soldiers exploited a gap in the Union line at the Brotherton Farm. Some of the Union army retreated, including its commander, William Rosecrans. The Union army was on the brink of disaster. Luckily for the Yankees, General George H. Thomas, a corps commander, rallied all the Federal soldiers

General George H. Thomas.

he could find and positioned them on Snodgrass Hill in an effort to prevent a hopeless rout. As individual Union regiments made determined stands and bought the army valuable time, Thomas set his men to work throwing up breastworks and strengthening his tenuous line. Thomas' efforts were tested in short order, with Confederate attacks beginning in earnest on Snodgrass Hill and the adjacent ridge at about 1 p.m.

Time after time the Confederates attacked the Union line, and time after time they were driven back with grievous losses. Thomas safely withdrew his men that evening. The field of battle belonged to the victorious Confederates, but they failed to pursue the retreating Federal army. Thomas' stubbornly courageous stand here at Snodgrass Hill had protected the retreating Union army from possible annihilation, and prevented Confederate forces from re-taking Chattanooga. Future United States president James Garfield, who was then a field officer in the Army of the Cumberland, reached Thomas during the battle, carrying orders from Rosecrans to retreat. When Thomas told Garfield he would have to stay behind to see to the army's safety, Garfield told Rosecrans that Thomas was "standing like a rock." As a result, Thomas gained rightful fame as "The Rock of Chickamauga."

Location: 3370 Lafayette Rd., Fort Oglethorpe, Georgia 30742

Drive the Atlanta Campaign
Northwest Georgia

Why? *The Atlanta Campaign of 1864 was the crucial development that many believe both confirmed President Lincoln's reelection and sealed the doom of the Confederacy.*

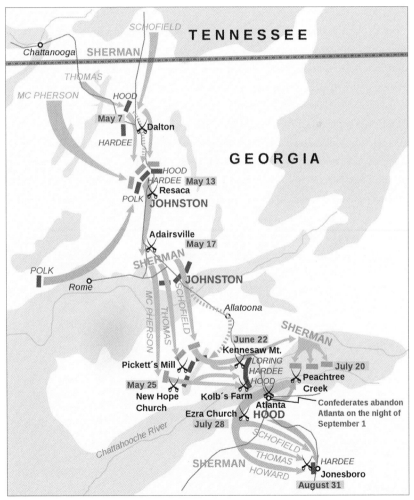

Make sure you have a good map before you take an Atlanta Campaign driving tour.

Description: By May 1864 it was obvious that the war was coming to Atlanta. Union General William T. Sherman was preparing his huge army to launch a major offensive against the city from his supply base at Chattanooga. Just a few miles away in Dalton, Confederate commander General Joseph E. Johnston readied his army to meet the offensive he knew was coming. Sherman began moving in early May, with the Confederates fighting, maneuvering, and slowing the dogged Federal advance. Sherman also fought and maneuvered, knowing it would be just a matter of time before Johnston ran out of time and space. By early July Johnston's men were pushed to the outskirts of Atlanta. Frustrated with the situation at hand, Jefferson Davis replaced Johnston with General John Bell Hood, who promptly launched several brave but costly offensives against the Federals. Hood was finally forced to abandon Atlanta on September 1, 1864, and the Union army occupied the city the next day.

To correctly follow the path Sherman and his men took to get to Atlanta, make sure you have good maps and a solid tour book in your car. While many locations are gone or inaccessible, just by following the route (mostly US Route 41) and stopping at select sites, you'll go through or by Ringgold, Tunnel Hill, Dalton, Resaca, Adairsville, Cassville, Cartersville, Allatoona, and Dallas. Make sure you stop at Pickett's Mill and Kennesaw Mountain—places listed elsewhere in this book—and possibly pull off at a place called Gilgal Church, which is very hard to find but worth it. Here a small reproduction fortification has been constructed at the site of a lively fight.

Location: Atlanta, Georgia, and vicinity

See What the Soldiers Saw at Pickett's Mill
Pickett's Mill Battlefield, Georgia

Why? Pickett's Mill is the pristine battlefield of the Atlanta Campaign that takes visitors back in time with its visual consistency.

Description: On May 27, 1864, the Union army attempted to outflank the Confederate position outside of Atlanta. More than 14,000 Federal troops under General O. O. Howard were handed the assignment. After an initial march of five miles, Howard's force reached the vicinity of Pickett's Mill where 10,000 Confederates under the command of Irish-born General Patrick Cleburne, who had already proven to be one of the finest officers in the Confederacy, were waiting to receive them. The Union attack came around 5 p.m. and continued into the night. At dawn, Cleburne's Confederates were still in control of the field. Howard had lost 1,600 men, while the defending Confederates had lost just 500.

The site of this Atlanta campaign engagement is incredibly well preserved. Roads, earthworks, and terrain features remain in a great state of preservation. See the media presentation and relics from the fight at the visitor center first.

Location: 4432 Mt. Tabor Church Rd., Dallas, Georgia 30132

The peaceful setting at Pickett's Mill belies the horror of 1864.

NOT JUST MEN

The Civil War is often defined by the stories of the individual men who fought it—Lee, Grant, Sherman, Jackson—but that definition is not complete without the stories of the women who took part in the conflict. While the depiction of the women left at home to sew socks and pine for their soldier husbands is not without foundation, it leaves out the more active roles that many women took.

If a woman wanted to contribute to the war effort, the most obvious job she could take on was that of a hospital worker or nurse. Prior to the war, most nurses were male, but with the shortage of manpower on both sides, women were eventually allowed into the hospital wards. The "mother" of Civil War nursing was Mary Ann Bickerdyke, who served as chief of nursing under General Ulysses S. Grant. Bickerdyke organized and set up hospitals and recruited young women to staff them. Clara Barton also started her career in nursing during the Civil War, serving in field hospitals and bringing supplies to the front; she would go on to establish the American Red Cross.

Rose Greenhow.

Those women seeking adventure often took on the role of spies. Rose O'Neal Greenhow conducted spy operations for the Confederacy and was credited by Jefferson Davis for all but saving the Confederacy at the battle of First Manassas. Elizabeth Van Lew took on the persona of "Crazy Bet" and spied for the North, often visiting Union officers held in Richmond's Libby Prison and smuggling out their messages.

Civil War–era women were also brave enough to participate in combat. There are more than 400 documented cases of women serving on both sides disguised as male soldiers. Some, like Sarah Rosetta Wakeman, who served as a private in the Union army, died in prisoner of war camps, their secret undiscovered until the very end. Others, like Loreta Janeta Velazquez, who served as a lieutenant in the Confederate army, were wounded and left the army on their own in order to prevent discovery. The true number of women combatants in the Civil War will never be known, as those who were successful in concealing their identity were rarely documented.

Vivandiere Mary Tepe at Gettysburg soon after the battle.

READ SAM WATKINS' ACCOUNT AT THE DEAD ANGLE
Kennesaw Mountain National Battlefield Park, Georgia

Why? *Although reading a first-hand account of a battle is often enlightening, reading Sam Watkins' words while standing at Kennesaw Mountain is truly moving.*

Description: After confronting General Joseph E. Johnston on numerous battlefields in north Georgia, General William T. Sherman was frustrated by his own slow progress and altered his tactics from that of maneuver to that of blunt assault at Kennesaw Mountain—a bad decision. Johnston's army was strongly dug in across the face of the mountain, twenty miles northwest of Atlanta. Sherman was confident that Johnston had extended his lines too thinly and, as a result, would be vulnerable to a direct assault.

After an artillery bombardment, 13,000 Federals charged Kennesaw Mountain. Though they initially made good progress, they soon found the attack utterly futile. The fighting was particularly intense at what was dubbed the Dead Angle. When the fighting ended around noon, Sherman

Confederate fortifications at Kennesaw Mountain.

had suffered some 3,000 casualties. As one Confederate remembered it, the Federals "seemed to walk up and take death as coolly as if they were automatic or wooden men." Sam Watkins, another Confederate soldier, left an incredible account of this battle in his memoirs : "I've heard men say that if they ever killed a Yankee during the war they were not aware of it. I am satisfied that on this memorable day, every man in our regiment killed from . . . twenty to a hundred each. All that was necessary was to load and shoot. Afterward, I heard a soldier say he thought 'hell had broke loose in Georgia, sure enough.'" This is just a small portion of Watkins' Dead Angle account. Make sure you have a copy of his book, *Co. Aytch*, with you when you go.

Location: 900 Kennesaw Mountain Dr., Kennesaw, Georgia 30152

Looking from the Dead Angle toward the scene of the Union attack.

Explore the Southern Museum
Kennesaw, Georgia

Why? This is an extraordinary museum in Kennesaw devoted to the daily lives of soldiers in the Civil War, with a special focus on railroads and the Great Locomotive Chase.

Description: The Southern Museum of Civil War and Locomotive History houses three permanent collections and boasts membership in the Smithsonian Affiliations Program. A wide range of exhibits offers a glimpse into the daily lives of soldiers, but the museum's standout feature is its impressive gathering of railroad-related artifacts from Georgia and other Confederate states, including a reproduction of a turn-of-the-century locomotive assembly line from the Glover Machine Works. The highlight of the collection is the *General,* the famous steam locomotive used in the Great Locomotive Chase in April of 1862.

The Archives at the museum contain company records, engineering drawings, blueprints, glass plate negatives, photographs, and correspondences from a variety of American businesses representing the railroad industry in the South during and after the Civil War, as well as a vast collection of Civil War letters, diaries, and other official records. This museum is truly a gem and a must-see when you're in the area.

Location: 2829 Cherokee St., Kennesaw, Georgia 30144

See the Atlanta History Center's Collections
Atlanta, Georgia

Why? *The sheer breadth and depth of this museum is only outshone by its absolutely incredible Civil War collection and exhibit.*

Description: The Atlanta History Center chronicles the history of Atlanta, Georgia, and indeed the entire Southeast, with a huge collection of photographs, maps, books, newspapers, furnishings, Civil War artifacts, and decorative arts. The center's thirty-three woodland acres include: self-guided walking trails, six gardens, one of the Southeast's largest history museums, two historic houses—the Swan House and the Tullie Smith farm—the Centennial Olympic Games Museum, and the Kenan Research Center. The Center's history museum focuses on the many ways in which Atlanta became the South's leading city, as well as on African American history, the Civil War, and *Gone With the Wind*, among other things. Its noted exhibition, *Turning Point: The American Civil War,* explores the Civil War in depth, particularly the Atlanta campaign of 1864, which was a major turning point of the conflict.

The museum's collection of Civil War artifacts is the largest in the state of Georgia and one of the five largest in the United States, with multiple collections consisting of more than 10,000 historic objects, including guns, uniforms, military equipment, and diverse memorabilia.

Location: 130 West Paces Ferry Rd. NW, Atlanta, Georgia 30305

EXPERIENCE THE ROTATING ATLANTA CYCLORAMA
Atlanta, Georgia

Why? *Don't miss the chance to see this epic depiction of the Battle of Atlanta, one of the largest oil paintings in the world.*

Description: At an astounding 42 feet in height, 358 feet in circumference, and 10,000 pounds, and covering a canvas area of more than 15,000 square feet, the Atlanta Cyclorama is a truly awesome painting of the Battle of Atlanta. Visitors are immediately surrounded by the cylindrical painting, which sits in place as the auditorium slowly rotates while music and narration complement the viewing experience. A short film, narrated by James Earl Jones, brings viewers up to speed on the campaign that culminated on July 22, 1864, with the Battle of Atlanta. There, Confederate soldiers under General John Bell Hood made one last attempt to save the city from encircling Union armies under Sherman. After vicious back-and-forth fighting through the day, Union troops eventually prevailed, and by the time darkness settled, 12,000 men had been killed, wounded, or captured. The facility also houses the locomotive *Texas*, which chased the *General* in *The Great Locomotive Chase*.

Location: 800-C Cherokee Ave. SE, Atlanta, Georgia 30315

The painting and its foreground exhibits blend together so well that it's difficult to tell where one ends and the other begins.

VISIT GENERALS AND MARGARET MITCHELL AT REST
Atlanta, Georgia

Why? Oakland is the final resting place of five generals, thousands of Confederate soldiers, and Margaret Mitchell, author of Gone With the Wind.

Description: Oakland Cemetery is the oldest in the city of Atlanta. Originally founded as "Atlanta Cemetery" in 1850 on six acres, it was renamed in 1872 given its many oak and magnolia trees. Since then, Atlanta's growth has rendered the cemetery near the city center. It survived the destruction of the city at the hands of Sherman and was the only active cemetery in Atlanta for thirty-four years after. More than 70,000 people are buried there: Confederate and Union soldiers (including five Confederate generals), prominent families, paupers, governors, mayors, golfing great Bobby Jones, and author Mitchell. There's also a Jewish section, a black section (dating back to the days of segregation), and a potter's field. The memory of the Civil War dominates the cemetery, especially the two beautiful monuments to the Confederate war dead. Standing at the marker commemorating the "Great Locomotive Chase," you can clearly see the trees from which Union soldiers were hanged for spying.

Location: 248 Oakland Ave. SE, Atlanta, Georgia 30312

NOT JUST WHITES

African American experiences during the Civil War varied greatly. Free blacks living in the North were faced with racism and inequality, but many still volunteered for service in the Union armies, despite a pervasive belief that they would be unfit for combat. In the early years of the war, many served in the military as laborers, cooks, and in other capacities, but following the issuance of the Emancipation Proclamation in September 1862, enlistment skyrocketed. By August 1863, more than a dozen "colored regiments" had been established and were ready for service. Although blacks could often be seen in Confederate units, they were serving as personal attendants, cooks, or even engineers. No black Confederate soldier is known to have fought in the Civil War.

The first combat seen by African American Union troops was at the October 1862 Battle of Island Mound, Missouri, when the 1st Kansas Colored Volunteers successfully beat back a Confederate attack. More widely renowned engagements soon followed. As shown in the Academy Award–winning film *Glory,* the

United States Colored Troops.

most celebrated action of U.S. Colored Troops was the 54th Massachusetts's vicious assault on Fort Wagner, South Carolina, July 18, 1863. Other particularly notable engagements for black troops included the July 30, 1864, Battle of the Crater and the April 12, 1864, fighting at Fort Pillow, Tennessee, where Confederate troops were accused of wantonly massacring the black troops.

Some 180,000 African Americans—both freedmen and runaway slaves—joined the ranks of the Union armies in 163 units of the Union army, while tens of thousands more served in the Union Navy. By war's end, these "colored troops" made up approximately 10 percent of Union military might. In all, more than 30,000 African Americans laid down their lives in the struggle.

USCTs pose for the camera at Dutch Gap.

Explore the Port Columbus Civil War Naval Museum
Columbus, Georgia

Why? *This is the premier museum interpreting the Civil War at sea and among the only places you have a chance to see, hear, and feel live firing of heavy Civil War artillery.*

Description: The museum at Port Columbus is the only one in the country dedicated exclusively to the often-overlooked maritime aspects of the Civil War. It boasts 40,000 square feet of exhibits, including a number of original Civil War ships, live firing demonstrations, numerous artifacts, flags, weapons, and uniforms of naval distinction. The museum proudly features rebuilt portions of the USS *Hartford*, the USS *Monitor*, and CSS *Albemarle*. The highlight, however, is the battle-experience theater and Confederate ironclad ship simulator, which situates visitors in the middle of a Civil War naval battle and brings the experience to life.

Location: 1002 Victory Dr., Columbus, Georgia 31901

TOUR THE NOTORIOUS ANDERSONVILLE PRISON SITE
Andersonville National Historic Site, Georgia

Why? *This was the site of the most horrific of Civil War prisoner-of-war camps.*

Description: Camp Sumter, more commonly known as Andersonville, was one of the largest and certainly the most dreadful of all the military prisons established by the Confederacy during the Civil War. Throughout fourteen months of operation in 1864 and 1865, it held 45,000 Federal prisoners. Of these, nearly 13,000 died of disease, poor sanitation, malnutrition, overcrowding, and exposure to the elements. It became one of the largest population centers in the entire South as its numbers swelled to 32,000 in August of 1864. And all these soldiers were held on fewer than twenty-seven acres of stockade.

Andersonville with its notorious "Dead Line" in the right foreground.

Andersonville has its own National Cemetery and is an active burial ground for contemporary veterans.

The site of the old prison camp is a national memorial to prisoners of war. The National Prisoner of War Museum, which opened its doors in 1998, tells the story of prisoner-of-war experiences from the American Revolution up through Afghanistan and Iraq and is dedicated to all of the American men and women who have ever suffered as POWs anywhere in the world.

Location: 496 Cemetery Rd., Andersonville, Georgia 31711

SEE THE LARGEST MONUMENT: STONE MOUNTAIN
Stone Mountain Park, Georgia

Why? *The Stone Mountain Civil War memorial is the largest single monument in the country.*

Description: The Confederate Memorial on Stone Mountain is worth seeing if for no other reason than it is the largest relief carving in the world, featuring a 90-foot-by-190-foot carving of Confederate president Jefferson Davis, General Robert E. Lee, and General Thomas J. "Stonewall" Jackson! Visit Memorial Hall, where exhibits featuring original designs, scale models, and the eleven-minute feature film *The Men Who Carved the Mountain,* show how this monument was created. Stand beside the full-scale replicas of some parts of the carving and then take the trail to the top of Stone Mountain for a spectacular view of the memorial, the city of Atlanta, and the surrounding countryside.

Location: 1000 Robert E. Lee Dr., Stone Mountain, Georgia 30083

NOT JUST BLACK AND WHITE

With a great focus upon women and African Americans, it would be easy to omit the important contributions of other important groups—Native Americans and Hispanics. Native Americans served en masse on both sides of the conflict.

While the number of Native Americans serving the Confederacy is unclear, nearly 3,600 fought for the Union in the east and, in particular, the western theater. Native American heroes emerged on both sides. Colonel Ely Parker, a member of the Seneca tribe and a trained attorney, was once rejected for U.S. military service because of his race. He eventually rose to serve as General

Col. Ely Parker sits among Grant's staff to the right of the door.

Grant's military secretary. On the Southern side, the most renowned Native American figure was General Chief Stand Watie. His 1st Cherokee Mounted Rifles fought at Wilson's Creek, Pea Ridge, and numerous other engagements near the Indian Territory. Unreconstructed to the bitter end, Watie refused to surrender until June 23, 1865, long after the majority of the Confederate leaders had capitulated.

Despite hopes to the contrary, Civil War service failed to improve living conditions for most tribes—quite the reverse, in fact, in many cases.

From the very first shots fired at Fort Sumter, South Carolina, in 1861, to the very last action at Palmito Ranch, Texas, in 1865, Hispanics played a role in the Civil War, contributing significant numbers to the cause. Of the approximately 27,500 Mexican Americans living in the United States, more than 3,500 joined the ranks, and two—Philip Bazaar and John Ortega—earned Medals of Honor for their valor in naval actions.

New Mexico Volunteers fought for the Union under Mexican American Colonel Miguel E. Pino at the Battles of Valverde and Glorieta Pass in early 1862. More Mexican American Union companies were raised in Texas and California, including 500 men of Spanish and Mexican origin in 1st Battalion of Native Cavalry. The highest ranking and most famous Hispanic to serve the Union cause was Admiral David Glasgow Farragut, whose Spanish father came to the United States in 1776 and fought in the Revolution and the War of 1812.

Hispanics also served with distinction in a variety of Confederate units, on foot and mounted, with names like the Louisiana Zouaves Battalion, the Spanish Legion of the European Brigade, and the Spanish Guard of Mobile, Alabama.

See 11-Foot-Thick Walls at Fort Pulaski
Fort Pulaski National Monument, Georgia

Why? *The fall of this fort was critical to the success of the Union blockade, and the manner of its capture helped to change the way forts were built.*

Destruction at Fort Pulaski.

Description: Fort Pulaski, a national monument, is located fifteen miles east of Savannah off of US 80 on Cockspur and McQueen Islands at the mouth of the Savannah River. In its time, it cost $1 million to build, took twenty-five tons of brick and eighteen years of work to finish, and was captured in just around thirty hours by Federal forces. The fort was pentagonal and replete with galleries and drawbridges that crossed the moat. The fort was completed in 1847, with walls more than 11 feet thick; Georgia forces took control of it right before the war began.

However, quick to realize its strategic importance, Federal cannons took it under fire on April 11, 1862, from more than a mile away on Tybee Island, and promptly overwhelmed its defenders. This powerful, early war display showed the effectiveness of rifled artillery—guns that had grooved barrels, which allowed longer ranges. Shells from that violent day are still embedded in the walls. This new type of gun would put an end to masonry fortifications once and for all. The visitor center has interesting exhibits of the fort's history.

Location: Tybee Island, Georgia 31328

Tour the South Carolina Confederate Relic Room
Columbia, South Carolina

Why? *Learn first-hand the important role South Carolina played in the Civil War at this fascinating, interactive museum.*

Description: Founded in 1896 to honor South Carolina's Confederate veterans, the South Carolina Confederate Relic Room and Military Museum is the third oldest museum in the state. Visiting the museum gives you the chance to learn about South Carolina's rich and distinguished military tradition, going all the way back to the American Revolution. In the Confederate Relic Room you can see exciting artifacts, including battle flags of nine of South Carolina's Regiments; the flag of the Union 2nd SC Infantry, composed of freed South Carolina slaves; General Micah Jenkins' Confederate frock coat, worn when he was killed in 1864 at the Battle of the Wilderness; Union General Judson Kilpatrick's letter calling South Carolina the "hellhole of secession" and vowing to wreak havoc as Sherman's cavalry commander; and an ever-growing collection of Civil War weaponry. A historical archives collection and a 19th and 20th century textile collection complement the Civil War artifacts, allowing the museum to interpret the political and social influences on South Carolina's military history.

Location: 301 Gervais St., Columbia, South Carolina 29201

The South Carolina
Confederate Relic
Room and Military
Museum.

SEE FORTIFICATIONS OF WAR: FORT MOULTRIE
Sullivan's Island, South Carolina

Why? *Some of the first shots of the Civil War were fired from here toward Fort Sumter.*

Description: From its early days as a Revolutionary War fort made of palmetto logs, through to its World War II defenses, Fort Moultrie was critical to American coastal defense, and played a major role in the American Civil War. Major Robert Anderson and eighty-five Federals initially occupied the fort before they moved on to Fort Sumter in 1860. From April 12–13, 1861, the Confederates positioned at Fort Moultrie fired on the Federals in Fort Sumter. Standing on the fort, you can see all the way to Fort Sumter and get an appreciation for the range of Civil War artillery, as well as an understanding of how important a strategic location it was to both armies. The film in the visitors center is a must-see.

Location: 1214 Middle St., Sullivan's Island, South Carolina 29482

Just one of Fort Moultrie's many artillery positions.

SET SAIL TO FORT SUMTER
Charleston, South Carolina

Why? As historic and iconic a place as you will find relating to the war, Fort Sumter is truly where the Civil War began.

Description: Resting at the mouth of Charleston Harbor, Fort Sumter is where tensions between the North and South finally erupted to start a civil war. On April 10, 1861, General Beauregard, commanding the provisional Confederate forces at Charleston, demanded the immediate surrender of the Union garrison in Fort Sumter. The commander of the garrison, Major Robert Anderson, refused. On the morning of April 12, Confederate batteries opened fire on the fort. But the Sumter garrison

Fort Sumter just a day after the fort's surrender. This is one of the first Civil War photographs.

was unable to reply effectively to this fire. At 2:30 p.m. April 13, after thirty-four hours of firing, Major Anderson surrendered Fort Sumter, evacuating the garrison the next day. The bombardment of Fort Sumter proved to be the opening (though bloodless) engagement of the American Civil War. After this battle, Fort Sumter was occupied by Confederates for the majority of the war.

The bombardment and subsequent actions, including the devastating siege of Charleston from 1863 to 1865, reduced Fort Sumter to one-third of its original size. Although it was repaired after the war, it was never rebuilt to its original size.

Starting your trip at the Fort Sumter Visitor Education Center in Charleston, you can view extensive museum exhibits that tell the story of the growing sectionalism and strife between North and South. A ferry ride is required to get to the fort. When you get there, you can visit an indoor museum that gives the history of the fort from its construction in 1829 through modern times. Walking in the fort itself allows you to understand why this location was so critical to the people of Charleston and the Confederacy. From the fort you can also see Morris Island, which the Civil War Preservation Trust helped to preserve with the city of Charleston in 2008.

Location: Fort Sumter Visitor Education Center, 340 Concord St., Charleston, South Carolina

SEE THE ACTUAL HL *Hunley* SUBMARINE
North Charleston, South Carolina

Why? *The HL* Hunley *is the first submarine ever to sink an enemy warship.*

Description: After sinking twice during testing, killing all of one crew and part of another, the HL *Hunley* was finally successful on February 17, 1864, when it rammed a fixed torpedo into the USS *Housatonic*'s hull, sinking it. The *Hunley* soon sank about 3.5 miles off shore. There it remained until discovered in 1995 and recovered in 2000. The *Hunley*'s story is one not only of the invention of submarine warfare, but also of the role of archaeology in helping us better understand the war. *Hunley* curators offer a guided tour where you can look down at the actual submarine as she rests in a 90,000-gallon conservation tank. You can also see artifacts found on board and watch a film about the recovery effort.

Location: Warren Lasch Conservation Center, 1250 Supply St. (on the old Charleston Navy Base), North Charleston, South Carolina 29405

The HL *Hunley* undergoing conservation.

SPEND TIME IN THE HISTORIC CITY OF CHARLESTON
Charleston, South Carolina

Why? *Figuring into the American Revolution, the Civil War, and much more, Charleston is among America's most historic cities.*

Description: Charleston is a spectacular city, and being there you can't help but soak up its history. Long before the Civil War began in Charleston, this port city enjoyed wealth unlike any other in America. Rice planters reigned in this city as landed aristocrats, while Charleston's shipping merchants gained their fortunes from slaves, rice, and cotton.

There are numerous ways to go about taking in the city. You can bike through the streets of the Historic District or you may want to take a walking tour or a carriage tour. Civil War–specific walking tours are offered throughout the year. Of course you'll want to take the boat ride to Fort Sumter and explore the fort where the Civil War started, but even standing near the Battery, where citizens watched the war's beginning, is a great experience. Whatever else you choose to do in Charleston (Rainbow Row, the Market, historic churches, Charleston Harbor, or the other three Charleston-area suggestions in this book), your visit will serve as both a history lesson and an experience.

Location: Charleston, South Carolina

No city retains more historic character than Charleston.

RUN THE BLOCKADE TO FORT FISHER
Kure Beach, North Carolina

Why? This crucial fort helped to protect Wilmington—the last open port to the Confederacy.

Description: Until the last few months of the Civil War, Fort Fisher's mission was to protect blockade-runners en route to Wilmington with supplies important to the survival of the Confederate army. By 1865, the supply line through Wilmington was the only remaining supply route open to General Robert E. Lee's Army of Northern Virginia. Fort Fisher was the largest of all of the seacoast fortifications that were protecting the last open port to the Confederacy. After a huge Federal amphibious assault, the fort finally fell on January 15, 1865. The end of the Confederacy was near.

The site affords wonderful views of the Cape Fear River and the Atlantic Ocean. By visiting, you will have the opportunity to tour what remains of the fort's land face, which displays a very impressive reconstruction of a thirty-two-pounder seacoast gun at Shepherd's Battery. Furthermore, a trail will lead you from the visitor center past the gigantic earthworks to the rear of the fort. There are also guided tours available along with the wayside exhibits that provide additional information. Other displays feature various items recovered from some of the sunken blockade-runners.

Location: 1610 Fort Fisher Blvd. South, Kure Beach, North Carolina 28449

Fort Fisher, North Carolina.

Tour Averasboro and Bentonville Battlefields
Dunn and Four Oaks, North Carolina

Why? These are two key battles that directly precipitated the end of the war.

Description: The Battle of Averasboro was fought on March 16, 1865, and saw badly outnumbered Confederates of General William J. Hardee's corps delay the left wing of Union General William T. Sherman's advance northward during his Carolinas Campaign. The battle took place on the 8,000-acre Smithville Plantation along the Cape Fear River. The temporary delay gave the Confederates enough time to relocate additional reinforcements for Confederate General Joseph E. Johnston's final offensive of the war, at the Battle of Bentonville, fought some twenty-five miles away on March 19–21, 1865.

On March 19, part of Sherman's force encountered Johnston's entrenched Confederates, who had concentrated to meet his advance at Bentonville. Late in the afternoon, Johnston attacked and crushed

Bentonville—largest battlefield of North Carolina.

the line of the Union XIV Corps. The Yankees just barely held on. Elements of the XX Corps were thrown into the action as they arrived on the field. Five Confederate attacks failed to dislodge the Federal defenders, and darkness ended the first day's fighting. On March 20, Union reinforcements arrived, but fighting was sporadic. On the afternoon of the 21st, however, General Joseph Mower led his Union division across Mill Creek into the back of Johnston's troops. Confederate counterattacks stopped Mower's advance, ending the fighting at Bentonville—the largest Civil War battle fought in North Carolina. During the night, Johnston retreated across the bridge at Bentonville. On April 18, Johnston signed an armistice with Sherman at the Bennett Place, and on April 26 formally surrendered his army.

Location: Averasboro: 3300 NC Highway 82, Dunn, North Carolina 28334

    Bentonville: 5466 Harper House Rd., Four Oaks, North Carolina 27524

SEE THE LARGEST SURRENDER: BENNETT PLACE
Durham, North Carolina

Why? *Appomattox may get all the credit, but Confederate General Joseph E. Johnston's surrender here was the largest surrender of the Civil War.*

Description: After the battles of Averasboro and Bentonville, and General Robert E. Lee's surrender at Appomattox, it became abundantly clear to Confederate General Johnston that his army could not continue to fight. Johnston requested a meeting with General William T. Sherman to discuss a truce. Johnston, with a cavalry escort, met Sherman at the Bennett Farmhouse. During the first day's discussion Sherman showed Johnston the telegram telling of President Abraham Lincoln's assassination. The two generals met again on the following day, April 18, and signed the terms of surrender. The terms, however, were rejected by the government in Washington as being too generous. The two generals met again on April 26, 1865, and signed the revised papers surrendering all Confederate soldiers in North Carolina, South Carolina, Georgia, and Florida. This agreement surrendered nearly ninety thousand men, the largest group to surrender during the entire Civil War. This was some seventeen days after General Robert E. Lee's surrender at Appomattox.

Location: 4409 Bennett Memorial Rd., Durham, North Carolina 27705

The Bennett Place.

TOUR A CIVIL WAR BATTLEFIELD IN FLORIDA
Olustee, Florida

Why? See where the largest Civil War battle in Florida took place.

Description: Federal commander of the Department of the South, General Quincy A. Gillmore, launched an 1864 expedition in Florida to secure Union enclaves, disrupt Confederate supply routes vital to the Confederate armies, and recruit black soldiers. Union General Truman Seymour was able to penetrate deep into the state, occupying, destroying, and liberating all while meeting minimal resistance. That is, until February 20, when he approached Confederate General Joseph Finegan's 5,000-man force entrenched just outside Olustee. Finegan ordered one of his infantry brigades to attack Seymour's advanced units but it

The Olustee Battlefield.

was quickly repulsed. Finegan fought hard until he committed his last reserves. Just then, the Federal line finally broke and began to retreat. But Finegan made no attempt to exploit this retreat and allowed the majority of the fleeing Federal forces to safely reach Jacksonville. The Confederates had been victorious. The 54th Massachusetts, depicted in the movie *Glory*, also added to their already considerable reputation that day, when they pulled a train of wounded soldiers by hand for five miles, until some horses could finally be found to pull them the rest of the way. This story of bravery and incredible strength became widely known all over the country. With 2,807 casualties, Olustee was the largest battle ever fought in Florida.

Location: US Highway 90, Olustee, Florida 32072

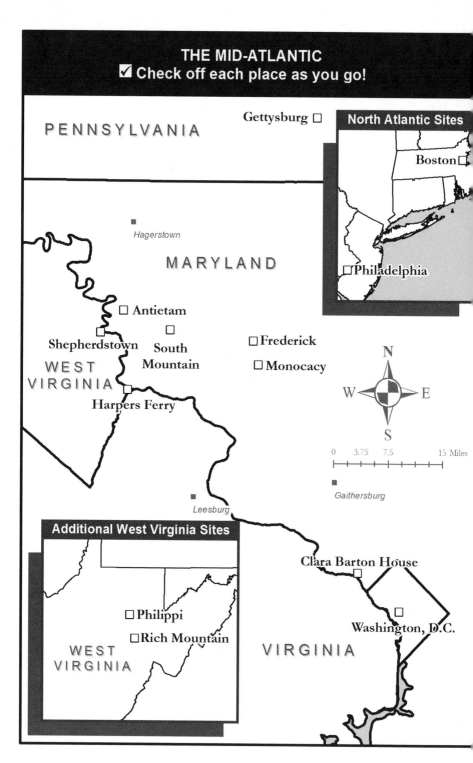

THE MID-ATLANTIC: D.C. TO WEST VIRGINIA TO BOSTON

The Middle Atlantic and the Northeast figured prominently in the story of the Civil War. In a relatively small geographic area, you can find many of the most famous Civil War sites.

Every Civil War traveler has to visit Harpers Ferry, West Virginia. John Brown's infamous 1859 raid on the federal arsenal there fanned the flames of sectional conflict. While you're in the Mountain State, check out the scene of some of the earliest Civil War actions, at Rich Mountain and Philippi. Head back east to the Antietam National Battlefield, where September 17, 1862, became the bloodiest calendar day in American history, but also allowed President Lincoln to issue his preliminary Emancipation Proclamation. Take a short drive north to Gettysburg National Military Park, site of the largest battle of the war and rife with essential experiences for the Civil War traveler. Here, President Lincoln delivered the Gettysburg Address, giving voice to many of the Civil War themes that still resonate today.

Aside from these obvious sites, the region is packed with so many others. See where Booth shot Lincoln and follow his escape route. Tour the fields at Monocacy—the Battle that Saved Washington. Visit museums to learn about Civil War medicine, nursing, and tireless efforts of African Americans. And make the trip to Philadelphia and Boston to see a horse's head, the final resting places of heroes, and a particularly famous memorial.

Visit Shepherdstown and Boteler's Ford
Shepherdstown, West Virginia

Why? *See where the Maryland Campaign penned its bloody postscript.*

Description: Immediately after the Battle of Antietam, Shepherdstown became a massive hospital for the wounded Confederates who made it across the Potomac. Both public and private buildings were employed as hospitals for the wounded, leaving one resident to refer to the experience as like an "awful dream." Elmwood Cemetery, which sits on the outskirts of the colonial town, has a large Confederate section in it; many of these dead were casualties of the Maryland campaign itself. Henry Kyd Douglas, one of the more famous staff officers of "Stonewall" Jackson, who penned the post-war account "I Rode with Stonewall," is also buried here. On September 20, 1862, the last major action to take place during the Maryland campaign occurred at Boteler's Ford, located approximately one mile south of town. Access to the crossing and battlefield is available on both the West Virginia and Maryland sides of the ford.

Location: Intersection of River Road and Trough Road, Shepherdstown, West Virginia

Shepherdstown Visitor Center: 126 East German St., Shepherdstown, West Virginia

Boteler's Ford—
key crossing
point on the
Potomac River.

STAND IN JOHN BROWN'S FORT
Harpers Ferry National Historical Park, West Virginia

Why? *Few other towns are as well suited to tell the story of the run-up to the Civil War—and the war's terrible consequences—as Harpers Ferry, the town that John Brown made infamous.*

Description: In 1859 this industrial town and site of the Federal Arsenal was the target of the abolitionist John Brown's famous 1859 raid. Hoping to seize a portion of the arsenal and arm a slave revolt, Brown and his men quickly lost control as they attempted to execute the complicated plan. Forced to barricade himself and some of his followers inside a fire engine house, Brown held his ground until a contingent of U.S. Marines, fresh from Washington, D.C., and under the command of then-Colonel Robert E. Lee, stormed the engine house—forever to be known as "John Brown's

The Engine House, later known as John Brown's Fort, sits just inside the arsenal gates at left.

Fort." Subsequent to his capture, Brown was tried for treason against the Commonwealth of Virginia, found guilty, and hanged in Charles Town, Virginia, on December 2, 1859.

The famous orator and former slave Frederick Douglass later declared that Brown's fight here began "the war that ended slavery." Throughout the war, Harpers Ferry found itself in the path of several campaigning armies. It was often used as the base of operations for Union advances into the Shenandoah Valley, and it was here as well that Stonewall Jackson achieved one of his greatest victories, in September 1862, when he captured some 12,500 Federal soldiers prior to Antietam. By war's end, Harpers Ferry changed hands eight times—leaving an indelible mark on the region and its people that is still felt today.

Location: 171 Shoreline Dr., Harpers Ferry, West Virginia 25425

Go to Philippi and Rich Mountain
Philippi and Beverly, West Virginia

Why? *These sites, which are located off the beaten track, to say the least, offer a glimpse into the earliest actions of the war and an opportunity to learn about the battles that put George B. McClellan on the map.*

Description: On June 3, 1861, the city of Philippi was witness to the little-known but first land battle of the Civil War. It also happens to be where the war's first amputation took place, on a soldier named James Hanger. Nearby Rich Mountain Battlefield preserves equally impressive hidden gems: Confederate Camp Garnett and a connecting section of the old Staunton–Petersburg Turnpike. It was here that Federal troops under the command of George B. McClellan, on July 11, 1861, defeated Confederates holding the pass over Rich Mountain. McClellan's victory paved the way for his ascendancy to overall command of the Union Army of the Potomac and also assured Union control of northwestern Virginia throughout the remainder of the war. Ultimately, these early battles allowed for the subsequent creation of the state of West Virginia in 1863—a state born of battle.

Location: Philippi: 108 North Main St., Philippi, West Virginia 26416
Rich Mountain facing the town square, Beverly, West Virginia

Out of the way, but worth the trip—Rich Mountain.

Visit the National Museum of Civil War Medicine
Frederick, Maryland

Why? *Ever wondered what happened to the wounded following a battle? Nestled in historic Frederick, Maryland, this museum tells that often overlooked and tragic story in profound detail.*

Description: By the end of the American Civil War, more than 600,000 soldiers had lost their lives and thousands more were maimed for life. Today the history of Civil War medicine is shrouded in myth and half-truths. However, the reality is that the Civil War soldier received a higher level of medical care and compassion than many of us now realize. The four years of war also launched an era of medical innovation and progress that is still felt today, particularly on the modern battlefield. At this museum, you'll learn that story and see some of the finest medical artifacts of the era.

Location: 48 East Patrick St., Frederick, Maryland 21705

These are some of the exhibits inside the National Museum of Civil War Medicine.

SEE WHERE WASHINGTON WAS SAVED: MONOCACY
Monocacy National Battlefield, Frederick, Maryland

Why? *In the summer of 1864, when Confederate forces came dangerously close to marching on the nation's capital, the Battle of Monocacy slowed them long enough to save Washington itself!*

Description: After moving north from Lynchburg through the Shenandoah Valley, General Jubal A. Early's Confederate army crossed the Potomac River at Shepherdstown on July 5–6, 1864. On July 9, 1864, a makeshift Federal force under the command of General Lew Wallace confronted Early's troops along the Monocacy River. Wallace fought, slowed, and was ultimately driven back by Early. Hearing of Early's advance into Maryland, General Ulysses S. Grant put the rest of the VI Corps on transports at City Point, and sent them as quickly as possible to Washington. Wallace's outstanding delaying action at Monocacy allowed General Grant just enough time to get these reinforcements to Washington to save the city from Early's men. Early ultimately made it to the outskirts of Washington on July 11, 1864, as veterans of the VI Corps began arriving in Washington just that evening. Outgunned and exhausted, Early retreated into Virginia. Washington was safe. As a result, Monocacy has been properly called "The Battle that Saved Washington."

Location: 4801 Urbana Pike, Frederick, Maryland 21704

Cannon in front of one of Monocacy's many well-preserved farms. Photo by Chris Heisey

CROSS THE GAPS IN SOUTH MOUNTAIN
Jefferson, Maryland

Why? *To learn why Antietam was fought where it was requires a trip to the scenic ridgeline of South Mountain, where Confederates fought a desperate delaying action to save their army.*

Description: The Battle of South Mountain, fought on September 14, 1862, was the bloody prelude to Antietam, and where some believe General Robert E. Lee's first invasion of the North was truly stopped. Any visit to South Mountain State Battlefield should begin with a trip to the battlefield's office at Washington Monument State Park, off Route 40. There, you can talk to a park ranger and get the information necessary to tour this complex and rugged battlefield of mountains and passes. Driving the battlefield is your best option—with opportunities to walk the ground at Turner's Gap, Fox's Gap, and Crampton's Gap. Be sure to stop in Burkittsville, Maryland, a small agricultural village at the base of Crampton's Gap, where structures that contained field hospitals still remain.

Location: 900 Arnoldstown Rd., Jefferson, Maryland 21755

In addition to the beautiful scenery at Crampton's Gap, you can also visit the impressive Civil War Correspondents Memorial Arch.

STAND INSIDE DUNKER CHURCH
Antietam National Battlefield, Sharpsburg, Maryland

Why? *Walking into this house of worship, battle site, operating room, and photo subject can be a profoundly moving experience–and a much quieter one than in 1862!*

Description: The Dunker Church was the meeting house of a small sect of German Baptist Brethren who believed in fully immersing their baptized converts—hence, they were commonly known as the Dunkers. The church itself was built in 1852 and served as an important landmark throughout the Battle of Antietam. Repeated attempts to capture this ground were launched by both sides. At the beginning of the battle, the high ground around the church was held by Confederate General Stonewall Jackson, who had positioned his 8,000 troops nearby early in the morning of the battle.

The Dunker Church, September 1862.

Texans under the command of General John Bell Hood and Union troops under the direction of General George S. Greene both fought around the church as well. Following the battle, the dead and wounded of both sides littered the grounds of this once peaceful sanctuary. Some of the most famous images of the Civil War, and among the first to show dead soldiers on a Civil War battlefield, used the Dunker Church as a backdrop. In 1921 an intense storm destroyed the original church, but a reconstructed one, using some of the original materials, was erected by the National Park Service in 1960.

Location: 5831 Dunker Church Rd., Sharpsburg, MD 21782

Modern view of the Dunker Church.

MORE TO SEE AND DO

Although the limitations of this book required only 150 entries, there are hundreds of other meaningful—we might say *essential*—ways to experience Civil War history. Some of these are listed below, and hundreds more can be found on www.civilwar.org.

Here are thirty-three more entries of the hundreds that should have been on the list but were omitted for lack of space. Visit our website for more than the following, admittedly cryptic information.

- Have your wet plate photo taken
- Use a great website like civilwar.org or Civil War Richmond (www.md gorman.com)
- See a Civil War road trace
- See Phil Kearny's death site at Chantilly
- See where the Civil War's first martyr was made, in Alexandria
- See giant earthworks at Fort Brady
- See a little known Bermuda Hundred site—Battery Dantzler
- Enjoy the historic city of Fredericksburg
- See a city risen from the ashes—Hampton
- Visit a peaceful pre–Civil War church like St. Peter's in New Kent
- Visit a site long gone such as Fort Mahone
- Pay respects at Stonewall Jackson's grave(s)
- Climb Fisher's Hill in the Valley
- Visit a James River Plantation like Berkeley or Westover
- See the Manassas Museum
- See where A.P. Hill was killed just as the war was ending
- See where Colonel Turner Ashby breathed his last
- See a real Wilderness surrounding the Widow Tapp Farm
- See the medical interpretation at Chimborazo Hospital
- Tour Shiloh's Hornets Nest
- Climb Shy's Hill at Nashville
- See Shiloh's start at Fraley Field
- See the coolest stronghold you've never heard of—Fort Rosecrans

- Tour the Parker's Crossroads Battlefield
- See an eternal flame at Gettysburg's Peace Light Monument
- Spend hours at the Gettysburg Museum and Cyclorama
- Explore the Shirley House and the Illinois Monument, Vicksburg
- Go inside the Vicksburg Courthouse
- See antebellum homes in Natchez
- Marvel at the Thomas Viaduct at Relay
- Visit Ulysses S. Grant's Home in Galena
- Find Leonidas Polk's death site on Pine Mountain
- Walk the Confederate attack at the Brotherton Farm

Ruins at Hampton, Virginia.

WALK THROUGH THE BLOODY CORNFIELD
Antietam National Battlefield, Maryland

Why? *Walking through Miller's Cornfield, among the most poignant and saddest places in America, will give you a sense of the terror that was Antietam.*

Description: On the morning of September 17, 1862, Union General Joseph Hooker's men began their ominous advance in the direction of the Dunker Church through tall fields of ripe corn. As the men came out of the southern end of Farmer Miller's fields, Stonewall Jackson's command awaited their arrival. With each step forward through the corn, Union soldiers fell as a result of Confederate fire. A storm of cannonballs, canister, and musket balls took a terrible toll on attackers and defenders alike. Just as Jackson's line showed signs of collapse, the famed "Texas Brigade" launched a counterattack that knocked Union General Hooker's I Corps off the field.

The Federal XII Corps next joined the fray, and the attack moved forward with Union troops ultimately retaking some lost ground. Eventually the fight for the Cornfield petered out as the battle's focus shifted elsewhere. In its wake, the three-hour clash left nearly 8,550 combined casualties. Hooker described the harrowing aftermath of the battle in a letter that still resonates today: *"In the time I am writing, every stalk of corn in the northern and greater part of the field was cut as closely as could have been done with a knife, and the [Conf.] slain lay in rows precisely as they had stood in their ranks a few moments before. It was never my fortune to witness a more bloody, dismal battlefield."*

Location: 5831 Dunker Church Rd., Sharpsburg, MD 21782

The Bloody Cornfield today.

Stroll the Length of the Sunken Road
Antietam National Battlefield, Maryland

Why? Both a defensive position and a trap—few other landmarks are as synonymous with Antietam as is the "Bloody Lane." No visit can be considered complete without walking this hallowed path.

Description: As the morning phase of the Battle of Antietam shifted to the center of the Confederate line, the focus shifted to a country road that divided the property of two local farmers. Instead of conveying agricultural goods, the sunken country lane served as a natural rifle pit for two Confederate brigades on that bloody morning. The Union advance on these entrenched Confederates started with General William French's II Corps division, followed by General Israel Richardson's division. Each assault in turn was repulsed with murderous Confederate fire.

Finally, after a considerable loss of life, Richardson's Federal soldiers turned the right flank of the Confederate line and began firing down at the road's defenders. Overwhelmed by their Union attackers, the Confederate line crumbled and the ground earned the title of the "Bloody Lane." At a high price to both attackers and defenders, the Union army finally seized this terrain before the battle shifted elsewhere, but not before the lane became one of the most hallowed pieces of ground in North America.

Location: 5831 Dunker Church Rd., Sharpsburg, MD 21782

The Bloody Lane, September 1862.

Charge across Burnside's Bridge
Antietam National Battlefield, Maryland

Why? *Gazing at the formidable Confederate position above and walking across Burnside's Bridge fills you with a sense of awe and respect for those Union soldiers who died under the harrowing fire of Southern rifles.*

Description: Spanning Antietam Creek, this simple stone bridge played a crucial role in the Battle of Antietam. Here, in this now-peaceful setting, a small number of Confederates under General Robert Toombs successfully held off multiple attacks by elements of the Union army attempting to take the bridge—and to take the Confederate flank as well. After a considerable amount of effort and casualties, Union forces seized the bridge and overwhelmed the Confederate defenders on the heights. Following a two-hour lull to re-form the Union lines and prepare for an advance, Federal soldiers climbed the hill, and in the process drove back Confederates in their path back toward Sharpsburg.

Had it not been for the timely arrival of Confederate General A.P. Hill's division, after a forced march of seventeen miles from Harpers Ferry, Union forces may have been able to destroy the Army of Northern Virginia. Instead, Hill's men drove General Burnside all the way back to the heights overlooking the bridge. Burnside's performance at Antietam is still considered one of the most controversial aspects of the battle today.

Location: 5831 Dunker Church Rd., Sharpsburg, MD 21782

Burnside's Bridge just days after the fighting.

FEEL COMPASSION AT THE CLARA BARTON HOUSE
Clara Barton National Historic Site, Maryland

Why? *Stepping inside Clara Barton's home brings you closer to this enigmatic leader and gives you an opportunity to learn more about the woman who started a movement based on compassion.*

Description: Clara Barton dedicated the majority of her life to helping people in need—both on the home front and on the battlefield. Her life of service started during the American Civil War. Glen Echo was her home for the last fifteen years of her life and where she resided when she helped found the American Red Cross. The house also served as the headquarters of the American Red Cross from 1897 to 1904. The museum tells the true story of her dedication, passion, and concern for those far less fortunate. The museum also has a collection of items once owned by Clara herself.

Location: 5801 Oxford Rd., Glen Echo, Maryland 20812

The Clara Barton House.

VISIT THE FREDERICK DOUGLASS HOUSE
Washington, D.C.

Why? *Frederick Douglass was a prominent abolitionist and key figure during the Civil War.*

Description: After escaping from slavery in Maryland, Frederick Douglass settled in New Bedford, Massachusetts. His friendship with William Lloyd Garrison and popularization of his autobiography, *Narrative of the Life of Frederick Douglass, an American Slave,* began a long association with the abolitionist movement that eventually led him to become a leader of emancipation efforts. Cedar Hill, the home of Douglass from 1877 to 1895, is a perfect place to learn about one of America's most well-known orators and abolitionists. Park Service tours are available year-round. Come and celebrate the man who once said, "I will unite with anybody to do right and with no one to do wrong."

Location: 1411 W St. SE, Washington, D.C. 20020

The Frederick Douglass House.

Go to the National Portrait Gallery
Washington, D.C.

Why? *Gaze into a portrait of a Civil War general or politician and you'll be gazing into the past.*

Description: Reading a Civil War speech or document can be a powerful experience—but seeing the face of the person who authored that document uniquely humanizes that experience. In the Civil War room at the National Portrait Gallery, you can do just that by gazing into the eyes of some of the Civil War's best-known personalities. Beyond the impressive gallery of portraiture, the museum also holds a fine collection of art depicting important events through the eyes of the artists and photographers who witnessed them. Connect with the past by seeing it up close at the National Portrait Gallery.

Location: Eighth and F Streets NW, Washington, D.C. 20001

The immense Civil War–era U.S. Patent Office, in the distance, now houses the National Portrait Gallery.

SEE THE AFRICAN AMERICAN CIVIL WAR MEMORIAL
Washington, D.C.

Why? More than 200,000 African Americans served as soldiers in the Civil War and many more assisted the war effort in their own way. Learn more about their often overlooked contribution.

Description: This memorial commemorates the service of the 209,145 African American soldiers and sailors, and their 7,000 white officers, who served during the American Civil War as United States Colored Troops (USCT). Incredibly, the memorial also features the 209,145 names in an engraved wall that circles the statue. The sculpture, known as "The Spirit of Freedom," is a nine-foot bronze statue sculpted by Ed Hamilton of Louisville, Kentucky, who completed the work in 1997. A nearby building is home to a museum that is an excellent stop for any student of the war. Housing a collection of photographs, newspaper articles, uniforms, and weaponry, the museum tells the story of these soldiers— some of whom began their lives as slaves.

Location: 10 and U Streets NW, Washington, D.C. 20001 Museum is located at 1200 U St. NW, 20009

The African American Civil War Memorial.

READ ELOQUENT WORDS AT THE LINCOLN MEMORIAL
Washington, D.C.

Why? In the words of Secretary of War Edwin M. Stanton, Lincoln now "belongs to the ages," but his words are as powerful as ever—and there is no better place to re-read his classic addresses than at this monument to his memory.

Description: Dedicated on May 30, 1922, to honor the memory of the 16th president of the United States, the Lincoln Memorial is located on the National Mall in Washington, D.C. Framed by a classic architectural design, this iconic monument features Lincoln seated at the center of the structure, surrounded by inscriptions of his Gettysburg Address and Second Inaugural Address on the marble walls. The memorial itself has been the backdrop to numerous speeches, marches, and protests—including Martin Luther King's "I Have a Dream" speech—a testament to Lincoln's legacy and importance in American memory.

Location: 23rd Street NW, Washington, D.C. 20242

SEE LINCOLN'S SUMMER COTTAGE
Washington, D.C.

Why? *Aside from the White House, Lincoln spent more time here as president than anywhere else. Take a trip to the cottage that hosted a president who led a nation at war.*

Description: President Lincoln's Cottage is located on a hilltop with a panoramic view of Washington, D.C. Designated a National Monument by President Clinton in 2000, President Lincoln's Cottage was Lincoln's family residence for a quarter of his presidency and is one of the most significant historic sites in the District of Columbia directly linked to Lincoln's presidency. The Cottage is located on the grounds of the Armed Services Retirement Home in northwest Washington, D.C., and has been restored by the National Trust for Historic Preservation. During his presidency, Lincoln and his family lived here from June to November of 1862, 1863, and 1864. The president used the residence for many important meetings as well as for relaxation and a place to ponder and debate decisions of national importance. It was here that Lincoln discussed the course of the war, his reelection, and emancipation. During your time at the Cottage, be certain to take the "Signature Cottage Tour," an innovative group tour in which a guide uses "historical voices" and images to bring stories of Lincoln and his family to life. The site also features several new exhibits that tell this interesting and overlooked story.

Location: Armed Services Retirement Home, 140 Rock Creek Church Rd. NW, Washington, D.C. 20011

The Lincoln Cottage. Photo courtesy John Richter

CIVIL WAR RAILROADS

Because of the vast distances separating armies from their supply bases and the widespread laying of railroad track, the Civil War became the first war in which railroads played a critical and deciding role.

When the war began in April 1861, the Union had a clear-cut advantage over the Confederacy: The North's nearly 22,000 miles of usable railroad dwarfed the Confederacy's 9,000 miles. Moreover, the Union had at its disposal the numerous locomotive and railroad builders, foundries, mechanics, and other suppliers necessary to keep the trains running. Meanwhile, the effective Federal naval blockade of Southern ports, which removed the option of transporting troops and supplies by boat, placed greater strain on Southern rail infrastructure. Worse still, the varying widths of Confederate railroads required train contents to be unloaded and then reloaded onto new cars at frequent intervals. Despite these difficulties, the Confederates were first to use railroads in moving troops to and from the front.

Railroads became obvious military targets, with Union and Confederate troops demolishing important track segments and bridges throughout the war. Confederate General "Stonewall" Jackson successfully destroyed dozens of loco-

Repaired railroad bridge in Virginia.

motives at the B&O Railroad yard in Martinsburg, now West Virginia, in May 1861. Other locomotives were later seized and put into Confederate service. Repair supplies—pre-assembled wooden parts and bridges—were gathered at staging areas for prompt delivery to damaged areas, dramatically cutting down on the time required for repairs.

As the war went on, railroads played an increasingly critical role. At the beginning of his campaign for Atlanta, Union General William T. Sherman trained men to repair railroad lines and keep supplies moving to the front. By the time they reached Atlanta, they were skilled enough to repair damaged track in only one or two days. Conversely, they were also experts in rendering Confederate rail lines beyond repair.

In July 1864, City Point, Virginia, situated at the confluence of the James and Appomattox Rivers and with a rail connection to the siege lines at Petersburg, became the headquarters of Union General Ulysses S. Grant. Previously only a small port, City Point became the largest Federal supply depot of the war, stocking food, clothing, and ammunition in mass quantities. Regular supply deliveries by rail enabled Grant to maintain his position around Petersburg, ushering in the end of the war.

Sherman's men became quite capable in tearing up railroads, such as here in Atlanta.

Visit the Sole Battle in the District: Fort Stevens
Washington, D.C.

Why? *Stand where President Lincoln came under direct fire and at the site of the only Civil War battle fought in the District of Columbia.*

Description: At the beginning of the Civil War, in response to the threat of a Confederate assault on the capital itself, engineers constructed a circle of forts and batteries around Washington, D.C. Fort Massachusetts was one of these early defenses constructed along the Seventh Street Pike, a road leading into and out of Washington. In 1863, its name was changed to Fort Stevens, in memory of General Isaac Ingalls Stevens, who died at Chantilly, Virginia. On July 11–12, 1864, as Confederate General Jubal Early tried to capture the city, Fort Stevens was the site of the only battle within the District of Columbia.

President Abraham Lincoln came out to the fort on both days of the battle to observe the attack and, for a brief period of time, came under enemy fire. On July 12, he was ordered to take cover, in all likelihood by Union Major General Horatio Wright. However, one story suggests that future Supreme Court Justice Oliver Wendell Holmes Jr., then serving as an aide-de-camp to Wright, yelled at Lincoln, "Get down, you fool!" The site is now maintained by the National Park Service. The remains of forty-one Union soldiers who died in the Battle of Fort Stevens are buried on the grounds in the nearby Battleground National Cemetery.

Fort Stevens.

Location: 13th Street NW and Quackenbos Street NW, Washington, D.C. 20011

GO INTO FORD'S THEATRE
Washington, D.C.

Why? *Few events in American history resonate as strongly as the assassination of the beloved Abraham Lincoln—see where this fateful event occurred and consider its legacy today.*

Description: Only five days after the surrender of General Lee's army at Appomattox Court House, President Lincoln and his wife attended a performance of *Our American Cousin* at Ford's Theatre on April 14, 1865. That same night the famous actor John Wilkes Booth, in a desperate attempt to save or revive the Confederacy, stepped into the Presidential box and shot Lincoln in the back of the head. Booth then jumped onto the stage in front of a half-stunned audience, and cried out "Sic Semper

Ford's Theatre still looks very much the same as it did 150 years ago.

Tyrannis," Latin for "Thus always to tyrants" (although some heard "The South is avenged!"), just prior to fleeing through the back of the theater. After the shooting, Lincoln was taken across the street to the Petersen House, a neighboring boardinghouse, where he died nine hours later. The home is now known as the House Where Lincoln Died and is also now operated by the National Park Service. During your visit, be sure to see the Ford's Theatre Museum. Along with other exhibits, the museum displays the Derringer pistol Booth used to carry out the attack, Booth's diary, and the original door to Lincoln's theater box. The museum also cares for several Lincoln family items, including the president's coat, the blood-stained pillow from Lincoln's deathbed, and several large and prominent portraits of the president.

Location: 511–516 10th St. NW, Washington, D.C. 20004

The box in which Lincoln was shot and from which Booth leapt.

FOLLOW JOHN WILKES BOOTH'S ESCAPE ROUTE
Washington, D.C., Maryland, and Virginia

Why? Retrace the path of President Lincoln's assassin as a nation scrambled to apprehend those responsible for this heinous crime.

Description: After launching his fateful attack on President Lincoln at Ford's Theatre in Washington, D.C., John Wilkes Booth fled the city, and, joined by accomplice David Herold, gathered supplies at the Surratt House in Maryland. Early on the morning of April 15, the same day Lincoln died, Booth and Herold stopped at the farmhouse of Dr. Mudd,

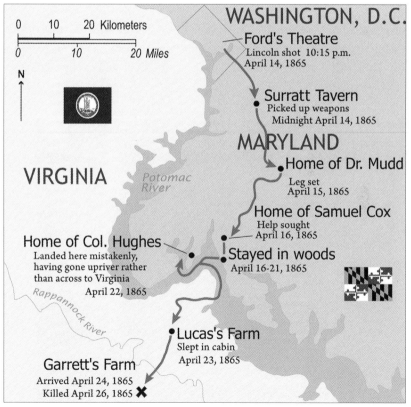

Make sure you have a good map before you drive the Escape Route.

who set and splinted the leg Booth broke when he jumped out of Lincoln's box at Ford's Theatre, forever linking the doctor to this infamous moment in American history. Booth and Herold hid for several days in a pine thicket before crossing the Potomac River into Virginia.

On April 24, Booth and Herold crossed the Rappahannock River and headed to Port Royal, Virginia, where they stopped at the Garrett farm. Federal soldiers, now hot on the conspirator's heels, soon found Booth's hideout at the Garrett farm. They surrounded a tobacco barn where Booth was sleeping and attempted to flush him out by setting fire to it. Booth was shot through the barn slats and soon died on the front porch of the Garrett house, ending his flight from Washington.

With interpretation provided by Civil War Trails, you can follow Booth's route on a driving tour that takes you to all the significant historic sites that were witness to Booth's escape. Unfortunately, your stop at the site of the Garrett House will be literally on a median strip between the lanes of US Route 1. Secure a solid tour map before embarking on your journey.

Location: Start at the Surratt House at 9118 Brandywine Rd., Clinton, Maryland

SEE WHERE THE ARMIES FIRST MET AT GETTYSBURG
Gettysburg National Military Park, Pennsylvania

Why? *Often overlooked in favor of the second and third day's fights, the clash on July 1st was just as desperate and arguably determined the outcome of the next two days.*

Description: The first day of the Battle of Gettysburg took place in three phases. First, two brigades under Confederate General Henry Heth attacked Union cavalry under General John Buford. As infantry reinforcements arrived from General John Reynolds' Union I Corps, these initial Rebel assaults were repulsed, although Reynolds himself was killed. By early afternoon, the Union XI Corps had arrived. With that, the second phase of the battle began as Confederates under General Robert Rodes attacked from Oak Hill and General Jubal A. Early's division moved in from the open fields north of town. The third phase of the battle began when Rodes renewed his assaults from the north and Heth and General W. Dorsey Pender joined in from the west. This Confederate assault eventually forced the Federal line to collapse. By the end of the first day, the Federals fell back through town and took up strong defensive positions on the ridgelines to the south of the Borough of Gettysburg. To understand Gettysburg, you must understand the clash of July 1st, which set the stage for the remaining two days of battle.

Location: 1195 Baltimore Pike, Gettysburg, Pennsylvania 17325

Mathew Brady and an assistant on McPherson's Ridge, July 1863.

Traverse Rocky Heights South of Gettysburg
Gettysburg National Military Park, Pennsylvania

Why? See the first two left flanks of the Union army during the fighting on July 2nd and why one fell and the other did not.

Description: The Union left flank hosted the most devastating fighting on the bloodiest day of America's bloodiest battle, and the Southerners struck Devil's Den and Little Round Top first.

On July 2, 1863, after Union General Dan Sickles moved his III Corps forward, the Union left flank was thinly manned between the Emmitsburg Road and the pile of boulders now known as Devil's Den. Around and atop the craggy Den, Union General John H. H. Ward's infantry and Captain James Smith's 4th New York Battery defended what was then

Looking from Devil's Den to the Valley of Death and Little Round Top just three days after the battle.

the left flank of the Army of the Potomac. It was an untenable position and, ultimately, Alabamians, Arkansans, Texans, and Georgians advanced through the rocks and overran the position.

Meanwhile, Union General Gouverneur Warren, Meade's chief engineer, discovered that Little Round Top was undefended and worked to get troops there. Through a complex series of events, Colonel Strong Vincent volunteered his brigade for the task. As the men from Michigan, New York, Pennsylvania, and Maine occupied the hill, Vincent ordered his regimental commanders to hold the ground at all costs. Vincent lost his own life in defense of the rocky hill. Twice, the Southerners almost captured the hill but each time they were pushed back just as success was within reach—once by the arrival of the 140th New York and then by a dramatic downhill bayonet charge by Colonel Joshua Lawrence Chamberlain's 20th Maine. The Union managed to hold Little Round Top, though at a heavy cost to both sides. The fighting at Little Round Top and Devil's Den produced more than 1,500 casualties.

Thanks to the park's recent efforts at battlefield rehabilitation, the view from the crest of both heights is nearly the same that Union and Confederate soldiers had on July 2, 1863, though peace has now settled over this once war-torn landscape.

Location: 1195 Baltimore Pike, Gettysburg, Pennsylvania 17325

THE IMAGE OF WAR

The Civil War was the first conflict to be extensively photographed, and it took the confluence of technology and capitalism to make it happen. The invention and dissemination of the wet-plate process, which, unlike the older Daguerreotype or tintype processes, produced a glass negative that allowed for images to be easily and inexpensively reproduced. The result was a market for portrait photography that inspired and helped to finance thousands of Civil War-era photographers. The overwhelming percentage of these worked in fixed studios and recorded and sold portraits, most commonly on small cards, known as *cartes de visite.*

A tiny percentage of photographers actually took to the field in specially outfitted lightproof wagons to record "documentary" photographs. More than 10,000 documentary Civil War photographs were recorded, and most of these were shot using a twin-lens stereoscopic camera which created dual images that, when placed in a special viewer, were bona fide 3-D photographs. These stereoscopic images were mounted on cards and sold by the tens of thousands.

A photographer in the field prepares a glass plate.

Among the first, great documentary photos of the Civil War—the wounded at Savage's Station.

Due to the scarcity of photographic supplies in the Confederacy, most documentary photographs were recorded by Northern photographers.

As the war progressed, photographers were able to inch further and further toward what we now know as photojournalism. In 1862 America saw photographs of field hospitals on the Virginia Peninsula, dead horses at Cedar Mountain, and finally, for the first time, dead soldiers on a battlefield, at Antietam. These images at once captivated and horrified the public. This was not the glorious image of war they had learned about. Rather, it demonstrated the loneliness of death and the distorted forms of soldiers. Many of these images were converted into woodcuts or engravings for widespread distribution in newspapers. Nonetheless, stereoview cards sold well and henceforth photographers tried to capture on glass plates images of dead soldiers on battlefields—an exceedingly difficult task only accomplished at six Civil War places: Antietam, Corinth, Gettysburg, Fredericksburg, Spotsylvania, and Petersburg.

Today the Library of Congress, the National Archives, and other institutions allow free online access to these priceless images—among the Civil War's most primary sources—that we can use to enhance our understanding of the conflict.

Dead horses at Cedar Mountain.

The photo-documentary goal achieved—dead soldiers captured by the photographer's lens on the battlefield at Antietam.

STAND ON AMERICA'S BLOODIEST PIECE OF PROPERTY
Gettysburg National Military Park, Pennsylvania

Why? This area hosted much of what Confederate General James Longstreet called "the best three hours fighting ever done by any troops on any battlefield."

Description: Until July 2, 1863, Joseph Sherfy's property was typical of most Gettysburg-area farms. But after fighting so horrible that Civil War veterans called it a "whirlpool of death," Sherfy's land was forever changed. His wheat field became *The Wheatfield,* his peach orchard *The Peach Orchard,* and his tenant farm *The Rose Farm.* Swept up by the intense battle, some 9,000 men were killed, wounded, or captured here. Fighting began on July 2 around 4:30 p.m. when General George Anderson's brigade attacked Union General Regis de Trobriand's brigade positioned on the southern end of the field. But that was the last time the numbers were anywhere near equal. As brigades from South Carolina, Georgia, and Mississippi entered the fray, they were confronted on average by two or more Union brigades from several Northern states. The pressure from the outnumbered Confederates was relentless and they claimed capture of Wheatfield, Stony Hill, Peach Orchard, the Rose Farm, and the nearby Devil's Den and Trostle Farm. But the numbers told the story, and the Confederates were stopped before breaking the main Union lines. The fight came to an end as darkness blanketed the field. The cacophony of battle subsided, save the screams of the wounded.

Location: 1195 Baltimore Pike, Gettysburg, Pennsylvania 17325

Confederate dead laid out for burial on the Rose Farm.

See Gettysburg's Important Flank: Culp's Hill

Gettysburg National Military Park, Pennsylvania

Why? In rear of the main Union line and commanding the critical Baltimore Pike, the Union defense of Culp's Hill was actually more important than that on Little Round Top.

Description: On the afternoon of July 2, 1863, the Union right flank was anchored near Culp's Hill. But just before the Confederates attacked the eminence, five of the six brigades of the Union XII Corps were ordered

The "Dead Tree Area" on Culp's Hill four years after the fighting.

to leave Culp's Hill and support the Union defense on the left flank. The remaining Union brigade, consisting of 1,400 New Yorkers under General George Sears Greene, stretched their lines and used recently constructed earthworks to hold off several thousand men of Confederate General Edward Johnson's division. The Yankees held the upper part of the hill, but the lower spire fell to Confederates. On the morning of July 3, both sides had reinforcements in place and the fight erupted at dawn and continued throughout the morning. The seven straight hours of fighting were the most sustained fight at Gettysburg and resulted in the Union holding the crest and recapturing the lower height.

After the battle, Culp's Hill's trees showed the severity of the fight, and its earth, rock, and log breastworks were there for years to come. This made Culp's Hill among the most popular sites to visit after the battle. Its popularity waned as trees died and the breastworks deteriorated, but there remains much to see on the hill, including roughly one mile of restored earthworks still visible at the edge of the tree line.

Location: 1195 Baltimore Pike, Gettysburg, Pennsylvania 17325

Walk the Fields of Pickett's Charge
Gettysburg National Military Park, Pennsylvania

Why? Put yourself back into the summer of 1863 and step off with the Army of Northern Virginia as they attempted to obtain a crowning victory in Pennsylvania—and learn why they failed to do so.

Description: At 1 p.m. on July 3, two Confederate cannon fired a signal. Just after, some 150 Confederate and 100 Union cannon roared to life. As the forty-minute artillery bombardment and duel came to an end, 12,000 men under Confederate General James Longstreet began moving forward. This massive line of infantry was suddenly showered with Union artillery that came roaring back to life. With that, explosions ripped through the Confederate ranks, and the men fell by the dozens. The Rebels, however, continued their charge toward Cemetery Ridge and the Union center. Despite their bravery, the Confederates were beaten back, and within an hour the assault had collapsed.

Looking from Cemetery Ridge toward the scene of the Confederate attack.

Today, when you come to Gettysburg and walk this same ground where so many brave men gave their lives from both North and South on that July afternoon, you can contemplate the legacy of that charge and what it meant for the men who made it—and repulsed it. The trail starts near the Virginia Monument on Seminary Ridge and takes you across a mile of open field, across the Emmitsburg Road and then to the Angle of two fence lines at the center of the Union line. This is where you will find the small grove of trees covering ground that will forever bear the name "The High Water Mark of the Confederacy."

Location: 1195 Baltimore Pike, Gettysburg, Pennsylvania 17325

SEE WHERE THE GETTYSBURG ADDRESS WAS COMPLETED
Gettysburg, Pennsylvania

Why? Stand in the room where President Lincoln put the finishing touches on one of the most famous speeches in world history: the Gettysburg Address.

Description: Arriving at the train station in Gettysburg on the evening of November 18, 1863, President Lincoln was escorted to the home of David Wills, where he spent the night and finished his address to be given the following day at the new national cemetery outside of town.

The David Wills House has several interactive exhibits and two rooms decorated as they were when Lincoln arrived, including a law office and the Lincoln Bedroom, where the President finished the speech. The exhibits in the museum present the story of this great battle's aftermath and what it meant for citizens and soldiers alike, as well as President Lincoln's visit to Gettysburg and his immortal Gettysburg Address.

Location: 8 Lincoln Sq., Gettysburg, Pennsylvania 17325

The David Wills House.

Visit Philadelphia's Civil War Sites
Philadelphia, Pennsylvania

Why? *Learn how Philadelphia supported the Keystone State during the American Civil War—support that was key to the Pennsylvania war effort.*

Description: During the Civil War, the City of Brotherly Love was an important source of men, money, weapons, and supplies for the Union war effort. More than fifty infantry and cavalry regiments were recruited fully or in part in Philadelphia, and the city's mills and depots churned out clothes for the troops. Along with the uniforms Philadelphia produced, the city's shipyards constructed numerous ships for the Union navy. Perhaps the city's largest contribution came in the form of medical care throughout the war. Philadelphia was the location of the two largest military hospitals in the United States: Satterlee and Mower. In 1863, during the Gettysburg Campaign, Philadelphia's leaders feared that Confederate forces might reach the city itself. In response, entrenchments were constructed around the city to defend against any direct assault. Fortunately, however, the Confederates were turned back at Wrightsville, Pennsylvania, and never came close to attacking the key to the Keystone State. Whether visiting Laurel Hill Cemetery, the Grand Army of the Republic Museum, or the Civil War and Underground Railroad Museum of Philadelphia, you will find plenty of Civil War–related things to do and see in Philadelphia.

Location: Philadelphia, Pennsylvania
Civil War and Underground Railroad Museum of Philadelphia: 1805 Pine St., Philadelphia, Pennsylvania
Laurel Hill Cemetery: 3822 Ridge Ave., Philadelphia, Pennsylvania
Grand Army of the Republic Museum and Library: 4278 Griscom St., Philadelphia, Pennsylvania

See the 54th Massachusetts Monument
Boston, Massachusetts

Why? *Pay a visit to the monument that honors the brave men of the 54th Massachusetts, the Civil War's most well-known black regiment.*

Description: Officially known as "The Robert Gould Shaw and Fifty-fourth Regiment Memorial," located across Beacon Street from the State House, this memorial serves as an eternal reminder of the heavy cost paid by the soldiers and families of this famous Civil War regiment. Designed by Augustus Saint-Gaudens and Stanford White, the bronze "Shaw Memorial" was unveiled and dedicated on Memorial Day, 1897.

It commemorates Colonel Robert Gould Shaw and the 54th Regiment of Massachusetts Volunteer Infantry, the group of men who made up the first African American regiment to be recruited from the North. Students of the war may also remember the 54th from the movie *Glory*, in which their storming of the fortifications on Morris Island, South Carolina, was dramatically portrayed, along with their recruitment and training.

Location: Boston Common (26 Beacon St.), Boston, Massachusetts 02108

The 54th Massachusetts Monument.

Virginia: Between the Capitals

$\mathcal{W}$ ith only 100 miles separating the Confederate capital at Richmond, Virginia, from Washington, D.C., the Old Dominion was destined to become ground zero for the Civil War's killing fields. From the Shenandoah Valley to the Tidewater, no region was spared from the bloodletting. Touring Civil War Virginia is a massive undertaking that can be made more manageable by examining geographic regions individually.

Learn about the first combat between ironclad warships and advance westward on the Peninsula like the Union army of 1862. Then, learn how emerging general Robert E. Lee sent the Yankees tumbling back from the gates of Richmond in the Seven Days Battles. See how General Ulysses S. Grant dealt with Lee a bit differently at Cold Harbor, Petersburg, and, logistically, at City Point. Follow Lee's army on the long road (and it is indeed a long road!) to Appomattox.

The Shenandoah Valley is host to numerous sites. From McDowell to the twin battlefields at Cross Keys and Port Republic, you can see where the Stonewall Brigade literally marched into history. In Lexington, see the final resting places of Generals Lee and Jackson, as well as those of their famous horses. Tour New Market to see where a corps of VMI cadets fought as a unit, and see the bloodiest battlefields in the Valley at Third Winchester and Cedar Creek.

Northern Virginia is also home to a wide variety of sites relating to nearly every aspect of the Civil War, from cemeteries to major battlefields to soldier graffiti. Fredericksburg and Spotsylvania County have so many essential sites that they could have their own 150 To-Do list. See the sites of many Confederate victories, see more Civil War artifacts than you've ever seen, and stand where some of the most historic pictures of the war were forever captured on glass.

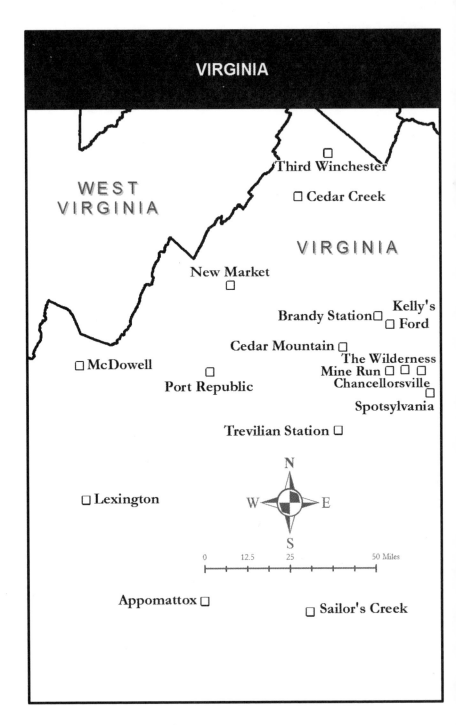

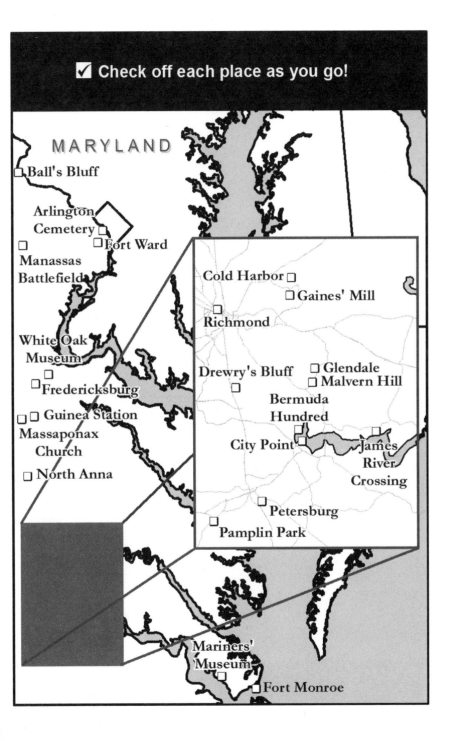

☑ Check off each place as you go!

Visit Arlington House and Cemetery
Arlington, Virginia

Why? *Once the home of General Robert E. and Mary Custis Lee, Arlington now serves as the largest and most well-known of the national cemeteries.*

Description: The 624-acre Arlington National Cemetery was established during the Civil War on the grounds of Arlington House, then the home of General Robert E. Lee and his wife, Mary Custis Lee. Mary Lee was Martha Washington's great-granddaughter. George Washington Parke Custis purchased the land upon which the cemetery now sits in 1802 and began building Arlington House. Eventually, the estate was passed down to Mary Lee and her husband. In 1861, after Robert E. Lee, then a colonel of engineers

Civil War burials. Arlington became so full that the aisles seen here have been used for interments.

in the U.S. Army, decided to resign his commission and join the Confederate army, he was deemed disloyal by most U.S. army officers. Thus, Quartermaster General Montgomery C. Meigs in 1864 proposed that two hundred acres of Arlington be taken as a graveyard for the Union dead. Until then, military burials were taking place elsewhere in the Washington area, but space was rapidly filling up. "We pray for those who lost their lives," Meigs wrote. "The grounds about the mansion are admirably adapted to such a use." Today, dead from all of America's wars are buried in the cemetery, from the Revolutionary War through the military actions in Afghanistan and Iraq. President Herbert Hoover took part in the first national Memorial Day ceremony at Arlington on May 30, 1929.

Location: 1 Memorial Dr., Arlington, Virginia 22211

SEE THE BEST-PRESERVED CAPITAL FORT: FORT WARD
Alexandria, Virginia

Why? *During the Civil War, Washington, D.C., was an armed camp bristling with fortifications. Fort Ward is the best preserved of this famous circle of forts that surrounded the capital.*

Description: Fort Ward was among the largest of the sixty-eight forts that once surrounded Washington, D.C., to protect the capital from attack during the Civil War. The fort was named after James Harmon Ward, the first Federal naval officer to die during the Civil War. Union General John Newton, who later served at Gettysburg, oversaw its construction, which was considered to be a superb model of military engineering. Liberated slaves, or "contrabands," helped build this and the other defenses around Washington. Today, Fort Ward is the best preserved of the forts, with about 90 percent of its earthen walls still intact. It is part of the City of Alexandria's 45-acre Fort Ward Museum and Historic Site. The museum offers a variety of exhibits on the Civil War and a very good Civil War library. The historic area includes a museum, an Officer's Hut, and a Ceremonial Gate. The reconstructed northwest bastion is a must-see stop for any visitor.

Location: 4301 West Braddock Rd., Alexandria, Virginia 22304

Gateway to Fort Ward.

SEE BALL'S BLUFF, A SMALL BATTLE WITH A BIG SHADOW
Ball's Bluff Regional Park, Leesburg, Virginia

Why? This small battle, fought along bluffs overlooking the Potomac River, had dramatic ramifications for the Union war effort.

Description: During the night of October 20, 1861, Washington-based Union General Charles P. Stone was ordered to stage a demonstration against Confederate forces across the Potomac River near Leesburg, Virginia. His assault was intended to distract the southerners from a Union thrust toward Leesburg from the Union encampments around Washington, D.C. Unbeknownst to Stone, however, the attack from Washington was called off and his men were on their own.

The site of Colonel Edward Baker's death at Ball's Bluff.

Confederates under General Nathan "Shanks" Evans launched a timely attack that caught Stone's men in a very vulnerable position, many of them still crossing the river. Evans drove the Union soldiers over the seventy-foot bluff and back into the river, where many drowned. This action also resulted in the capture of more than 700 Federal soldiers and the death of Colonel Edward D. Baker, a U.S. Senator and longtime friend of President Lincoln's. The embarrassing Union defeat led to Stone's arrest and the creation of the Congressional Joint Committee on the Conduct of the War, a politically powerful committee that kept senior Union commanders looking over their shoulders for the remainder of the war. Although hindsight tells us that Ball's Bluff was a small and relatively insignificant military action, the events that transpired there cast a long shadow over the Union war effort.

Location: Ball's Bluff Road, Leesburg, Virginia 20176

Take the Henry Hill Walking Tour
Manassas National Battlefield, Virginia

Why? Walk the ground of the first significant land battle of the Civil War.

Description: On July 21, 1861, the armies of North and South first clashed on the field of battle. Both were armies of amateurs, and few on either side had any idea what to expect when the Battle of Manassas (or First Bull Run) started that morning. At first, the Union army was winning, and appeared close to ending the brief rebellion. However, the tide of battle changed as the two armies met on Henry Hill.

Battlefield graves from the first battle, photographed in March 1862.

The terrain and tree lines have changed little since that fateful day. As you walk the one-mile Henry Hill loop trail, you will follow in the footsteps of the charging Union and Confederate troops and stand where Confederate General Thomas Jackson earned his sobriquet, "Stonewall." Try to imagine how the young men must have felt, exhausted and experiencing war for the first time, with cannon booms ringing in their ears as shell fragments and bullets flew around them. Some of the bloodiest fighting took place over possession of Ricketts' Union battery, located only a few steps from the visitor center. At sites along the trail, you will find interpretive signs that portray the men and events that decided the outcome of the Civil War's first major battle. If time allows, make sure you visit the many other sites associated with First Manassas, including the Stone Bridge, Sudley Ford, and Matthews Hill.

Location: 6511 Sudley Rd., Manassas, Virginia 20109

STAND IN THE DEEP CUT AT SECOND MANASSAS
Manassas National Battlefield, Virginia

Why? *This beautifully preserved part of the battlefield was the scene of repeated Union attacks on August 29 and 30, 1862.*

Description: In August 1862, General Robert E. Lee launched an offensive against the Union Army of Virginia, led by General John Pope. General Thomas "Stonewall" Jackson damaged Pope's supply lines and then waited for him at a carefully selected position near the old Manassas Battlefield. Jackson's line boasted the ready-made breastwork of an unfinished railroad cut, sweeping fields of fire, and easy road access to the other half of the army. When Pope couldn't find him, Jackson attacked a wing of the Union army on August 28, daring Pope to attack him.

The Deep Cut at Second Manassas.

Pope obliged, and engaged in a series of piecemeal attacks on August 29 and 30 against Jackson's formidable line. The most intense fighting occurred here at Deep Cut, where Union soldiers and Confederates engaged in desperate hand-to-hand fighting with bayonets and clubbed muskets. At one point, Jackson's men ran out of ammunition and resorted to throwing rocks. Massed Confederate artillery made the position untenable for the Federals. Unable to sustain the assault, the Yankees had no choice but to surrender or withdraw through a horrible shower of artillery. Jackson's stand here enabled Lee to mass the remainder of his army on the unprotected Union left flank. The resulting attack nearly destroyed Pope's army, and left it reeling in retreat toward Washington, D.C.

Today, a loop trail allows visitors to retrace the Union attack on Deep Cut. The fight here is best understood by following the park's Second Manassas driving tour, which will include stops at the Brawner Farm, Chinn Ridge, and more.

Location: 6314 Featherbed Lane, Gainesville, Virginia 20155

SEE KELLY'S FORD, WHERE THE GALLANT PELHAM FELL
Near Remington, Virginia

Why? Bucolic Kelly's Ford was the scene of a clash between opposing cavalry in March 1863. It is also where the dashing Confederate artilleryman John Pelham was fatally wounded.

Description: While the infantrymen of both armies encamped near Fredericksburg, restless cavalrymen in blue and gray converged on the Rappahannock River crossing at Kelly's Ford on March 17, 1863. General William Averell's Federal troopers crossed Kelly's Ford with orders to find and destroy General Fitzhugh Lee's elite brigade of Virginia cavalry. During nearly twelve hours of combat, Averell's division successfully drove the Virginians back some two miles along present-day Route 674 toward Brandy Station, before retiring back across the Rappahannock. For the Confederates, the battle was particularly painful because of the loss of John Pelham, a youthful artillery commander known as "the Gallant Pelham." The fatally wounded Pelham was brought to the home of his fiancée in Culpeper where he died later that day.

Location: 6370–6446 Edwards Shop Rd., Elkwood, Virginia 22734

SEE THE GRAFFITI HOUSE'S GRAFFITI
Brandy Station, Virginia

Why? The *"Graffiti House"* gets its name from the drawings left on its walls by soldiers convalescing in this makeshift hospital.

Description: Any trip to the Brandy Station battlefield must include a visit to the "Graffiti House." Built in 1858, the Graffiti House is one of the very few extant Civil War structures on the Brandy Station battlefield. Because of the house's proximity to the Orange & Alexandria Railroad and the Carolina Road, it saw frequent use by the Union and Confederate armies throughout the war. During the 1863 battle of Brandy Station, the Graffiti House served as a makeshift field hospital. It also served as a headquarters for federal troops stationed in the vicinity during the Union occupation of Culpeper County in the winter of 1863–1864. Soldiers from both sides made numerous drawings on the walls throughout the war, often proudly adding their names and unit designations to their writings. After the war, the owners of the building painted and papered over the graffiti, which was forgotten for more than a century. The graffiti was rediscovered during a 1993 renovation of the house, and much of it is on display today. The house serves as the headquarters of the nonprofit Brandy Station Foundation and as a visitor center for the battlefield.

Location: 19484 Brandy Rd., Brandy Station, Virginia 22714

Despite the vast array of graffiti visible, there is much more yet to be uncovered.

Stand Atop Buford's Knoll at Brandy Station
Brandy Station Battlefield, Virginia

Why? *Standing at this incredibly peaceful spot on the largest cavalry battlefield of the North American continent brings you back in time. The site, which also hosted the largest Union winter encampment of the war, remains in an almost pristine state of preservation.*

Description: Brandy Station is best known as the battle that "made the Union cavalry." After two years of being bested by their counterparts in gray, the Federal troopers were finally able to demonstrate they could hold their own in battle. The battle began in the early morning hours of June 9, 1863, when Federal cavaliers under Generals John Buford and David Gregg splashed across the Rappahannock River to engage Confederate cavalry encamped near the railroad station at Brandy. Confederate General W.H.F. "Rooney" Lee pulled his forces out of the fight with Buford's troopers over the stone wall that separated the Cunningham and Green farms. Lee's men fell back in a fighting retreat to Yew Ridge

Standing here, one can hardly fathom that this hallowed place almost became a race track.

and the most prominent terrain feature of the battlefield, Fleetwood Hill. The steep rolling topography combined with the charges and counter-charges along Fleetwood Hill tired out the mounts of the pursuing Federals. As a result, towards the end of the afternoon, Buford had determined that his men and their horses were too exhausted to continue fighting. Also, a fresh brigade of Confederate cavalry under Colonel Thomas Munford menaced Buford's retreat route across the Rappahannock. Buford thus decided to pull back to the far side of the river, giving the field to the Confederate troopers. By holding the field the Confederates claimed victory, but it was obvious to all engaged in the desperate encounter that the Union cavalry was now a force to be reckoned with.

Location: Beverly Ford Road, Brandy Station, Virginia 22714

TOUR THE CEDAR MOUNTAIN BATTLEFIELD
South of Culpeper, Virginia

Why? The battle of Cedar Mountain marked the opening salvo of the 1862 Second Manassas Campaign and the only time Stonewall Jackson drew his sword in battle.

Description: In June 1862, Union General John Pope was placed in command of the newly constituted Army of Virginia, with orders to operate along the vital Orange and Alexandria Railroad in Culpeper and Orange Counties. Confederate General Robert E. Lee responded to this new threat by sending General Thomas "Stonewall" Jackson and 14,000 men to Gordonsville. In early August, Pope marched his forces south with the intent of occupying Gordonsville. Jackson countered by attacking Pope's vanguard and then pushed across the Rapidan River toward Culpeper Courthouse.

Cedar Mountain looms above Union officers amidst battlefield graves.

The two armies clashed on August 9 under the shadow of Cedar Mountain. The Federals gained an early advantage and threatened to break the Southern line. At this pivotal moment, an excited Jackson uncharacteristically tried to brandish his sword. However, he used his sword so infrequently that it had become rusted to its scabbard, leaving him little choice but to wave both above his head. Whether inspired by Jackson or not, a counterattack by Confederate General A. P. Hill beat back the Federals and won the day. Pope's army had begun a retreat that led back to the battlefield of Manassas, where Lee and Jackson would inflict an even greater defeat on the hapless Union commander.

Location: 9521 General Winder Rd., Rapidan, Virginia 22733

The Civil War Trust's walking trail goes very near the site of the image on the previous page.

Stand in Awe at the White Oak Museum
Falmouth, Virginia

Why? *If you are fascinated with relics of the Civil War, the White Oak Museum is a must-see place. You will not see more Civil War artifacts on display anywhere.*

Description: The White Oak Civil War Museum is a hidden gem in Stafford County, Virginia. Although Stafford County did not host any big battles, its close proximity to waterways and railroad lines spurred Federal and Confederate encampments, minor skirmishes, major supply routes, and other important operations of war. Specifically, the museum is located near Belle Plain and the Union VI Corps camp where 20,000 soldiers lived during the winter of 1862–1863. Decades of artifact recovery from the area has resulted in an impressive array of Civil War artifacts—so many, in fact, it boggles the mind. Literally hundreds of thousands of Civil War bullets, hundreds of belt buckles and buttons, replicas and parts of actual wooden winter huts, and every implement of war that a soldier used is packed into the rather small museum. Enthusiastic and knowledgeable staff members are on site for interpretation and research.

Location: 985 White Oak Rd., Falmouth, Virginia 22405

Visit the House and Grounds at Chatham Manor
Fredericksburg and Spotsylvania National Military Park, Virginia

Why? *This Georgian-style manor, on a bluff overlooking the Rappahannock River, was a Union artillery position, headquarters, camp, and hospital, and it provides a panoramic view of historic Fredericksburg.*

Description: Chatham is an imposing, 180-foot-long brick manor house on a bluff overlooking the city of Fredericksburg and the Rappahannock River. Although best known for its Civil War connections, Chatham's history spans nearly 250 years. George Washington and Thomas Jefferson both spent time at Chatham, as did Abraham Lincoln, Clara Barton, and Walt Whitman. In December 1862, during the battle of Fredericksburg, Chatham served as a Union army headquarters, and Union guns situated on the grounds of Chatham fired into Confederate-occupied Fredericksburg, devastating much of the town.

Chatham Manor.

Although out of range of Confederate fire, Chatham itself was also devastated—while generals frantically issued orders from the porch, soldiers and wagons destroyed the once trim gardens, and surgeons turned the building's interior into a major field hospital. At least 130 Union soldiers died at Chatham and were buried on the grounds. Five months later, during the Chancellorsville Campaign, Chatham once again became a field hospital. It took decades for the area to recover. Today, Chatham is part of the Fredericksburg and Spotsylvania National Military Park and serves as the park's headquarters. The buildings and grounds are open daily, and five of the ten rooms hold exhibits. Make sure you walk out to the Rappahannock overlook to see the pontoon boat exhibit.

Location: 120 Chatham Lane, Fredericksburg, Virginia 22405

Stand in the Sunken Road at Fredericksburg
Fredericksburg and Spotsylvania National Military Park, Virginia

Why? *Wave after wave of Union soldiers charged against this position in one of the most lopsided engagements of the Civil War.*

Description: As you stand here and gaze at what remains of the Sunken Road that once linked Washington, D.C., and Richmond, it is easy to see how it earned its name. Cut into the base of imposing Marye's Heights, it sits several feet below the grade of the surrounding hill slope with stone retaining walls holding the banks in place and forming a ready-made trench for the Confederate army. On December 13, 1862, during the Battle of Fredericksburg, Confederate soldiers under General Robert E. Lee fired from this position upon multitudes of Union soldiers advancing from the direction of Fredericksburg. Behind the Confederate infantry in the Sunken Road, guns of the Washington Artillery were positioned on Marye's heights. Confederate artillerists fired over the heads of their comrades and scoured the plain before them. Although it had its weaknesses, the site is considered by many to be the strongest natural position Lee's army ever defended.

Location: 1013 Lafayette Blvd., Fredericksburg, Virginia 22401

The Sunken Road, photographed just minutes after the Union troops stormed it in May 1863.

SEE THE DECISIVE SLAUGHTER PEN FARM
Fredericksburg, Virginia

Why? *Although other parts of the Fredericksburg battlefield are better known, the Slaughter Pen Farm is where the battle was decided.*

Description: In December 1862, the Union Army of the Potomac began another march toward Richmond. The army's new commander, General Ambrose Burnside, hoped to steal a march on his opponent, General Robert E. Lee, and block his way at Fredericksburg. The late arrival of pontoons boats, however, prevented Burnside from making an uncontested crossing of the Rappahannock River. Once across the river, his army confronted a united Confederate army dug in along a seven-mile front. Burnside chose to attack Lee's army at two points: just outside the town against the Sunken Road below Marye's Heights, and at the Slaughter Pen Farm. Union General William B. Franklin, commanding the Union Left

One of the Civil War Trust's greatest preservation victories—the Slaughter Pen Farm.

Grand Division, was chosen to lead the attack across the Slaughter Pen Farm toward the Confederate right flank at Prospect Hill. Although he had 65,000 men at his disposal, he deployed only two divisions, numbering approximately 8,000 men, under Generals George Meade and John Gibbon. Meade's division successfully penetrated a large gap in the Confederate line but did not receive the necessary reinforcements in time to exploit his breakthrough. Gibbon's men were able to breach part of the Confederate line, but were also driven back because of a lack of support. The twin repulse deprived the Federal army of its only true chance of victory at Fredericksburg. Today, the Slaughter Pen Farm walking trail allows visitors to walk in the footsteps of Meade and Gibbon's men.

Location: 11196 Tidewater Trail, Fredericksburg, Virginia 22408

Tour the Chancellorsville Battlefield
Fredericksburg and Spotsylvania National Military Park, Virginia

Why? *Although it was Confederate General Robert E. Lee's greatest victory, the Battle of Chancellorsville came at the loss of Lee's greatest lieutenant, General Thomas "Stonewall" Jackson.*

Description: In late April 1863, Union General Joseph Hooker launched a bold flanking movement across the Rappahannock and Rapidan Rivers in an effort to outmaneuver Confederate General Robert E. Lee. Using the Germanna and Ely's Fords to cross the Rapidan, the Federals arrived at Chancellorsville on April 30 and May 1, successfully landing in the rear of Lee's Army. However, rather than retreat, Lee did the unexpected, attacking Hooker's larger army and forcing it back to a defensive position at Chancellorsville. On the morning of May 2, Lee's most trusted lieutenant, "Stonewall" Jackson, led 27,000 men on a march against the unprotected Union right flank. The resulting attack crushed the Federal XI Corps.

Right near the site of the Chancellorsville Visitor Center, check out two monuments to Stonewall Jackson's wounding.

However, later that night, while doing reconnaissance in front of his lines, Jackson's own men shot him accidentally. He was borne from the field, and cavalry chieftain J. E. B. Stuart took temporary command of his corps.

On May 3, the Confederates continued their attacks and broke the Federal line at Chancellorsville. Hooker and his army retreated one mile and then entrenched in a defensive "V" with their backs to the river at United States Ford. During the night of May 5–6, 1863, Hooker retreated back across the Rappahannock River. Lee's smaller force had just won another victory in one of the Civil War's bloodiest battles. Many historians consider Chancellorsville to be Lee's greatest victory, but his army never recovered from the loss of Stonewall Jackson, who died of his wounds on May 10, 1863.

Before you start your tour of Chancellorsville, stop at the Visitor Center, where you can get battlefield maps, buy an audio tour, and watch an introductory movie about the clash. Make sure to see Fairview, Hazel Grove, the scene of Jackson's flank attack, and the First Day's battlefield.

Location: 9001 Plank Rd., Spotsylvania, Virginia 22407

Chancellorsville Battlefield.

STAND AT THE CHANCELLOR HOUSE RUINS
Fredericksburg and Spotsylvania National Military Park, Virginia

Why? *The brick foundation is all that remains of the Chancellor House, the scene of one of the most dramatic moments of the Civil War.*

Description: Only the brick foundation remains of the Chancellor House, a roadside tavern and inn that is forever linked to the May 1863 battle of Chancellorsville. Here was the Union army headquarters and where Union commander Joseph Hooker was wounded and knocked out of action for several crucial hours during the battle. The house also saw one of the most dramatic moments of the Civil War: Robert E. Lee, flushed with victory and sitting on his favorite horse, Traveller, was cheered by thousands of Confederate troops who raised their hats to Lee in triumph. Wrote one Confederate staff officer, "It must have been from such a scene that men in ancient days rose to the dignity of gods."

Location: 8801 Elys Ford Rd., Fredericksburg, Virginia 22407

The burned out shell of the Chancellor House.

CROSS OVER THE RIVER TO GUINEA STATION
Guinea Station, Virginia

Why? *Visit the modest white clapboard building known as the Stonewall Jackson Shrine where the famous general crossed "over the river."*

Description: On May 2, 1863, following his famous flank attack at Chancellorsville that crushed the Union right flank, General Thomas "Stonewall" Jackson was wounded by his own men. At the time, Jackson was perhaps the most famous commander in the world, even eclipsing the fame of his commander, Robert E. Lee. His wounds did not seem mortal, but did necessitate the amputation of his left arm. Lee, worried that Jackson was recuperating at a site exposed to capture by the Union army, ordered that Jackson be moved to Guinea Station on the Richmond, Fredericksburg and Potomac Railroad. However, the twenty-seven-mile trip by ambulance to Guinea Station weakened Jackson, and pneumonia set in. Although his spirits were raised by a visit from his wife and newborn daughter, it soon became clear that Jackson was dying. In his final hours, Jackson frequently drifted into delirium, ordering his subordinate A. P. Hill into action. His final words were "Let us cross over the river and rest under the shade of the trees." He died at 3:15 p.m. on May 10. With him died many of the hopes of an independent Southern nation. The house is part of the Fredericksburg and Spotsylvania National Military Park.

Location: 12019 Stonewall Jackson Rd., Woodford, Virginia 22580

Stonewall Jackson's Shrine.

Visit Ellwood in the Wilderness
Fredericksburg and Spotsylvania National Military Park, Virginia

Why? *The stately home of the Lacy family served as a field headquarters during two separate battles and is the final resting place of the legendary Stonewall Jackson's left arm.*

Description: Ellwood, located amidst the stunted trees and densely tangled undergrowth of the Wilderness, served as Union V Corps commander Gouverneur Warren's headquarters during the battle on May 5–7, 1864. Carefully restored through volunteer efforts, the home's interior features several exhibits to explore. No trip to Ellwood would be complete without a visit to the Lacey family cemetery on the property, where Stonewall Jackson's left arm was interred following its amputation at nearby Wilderness Tavern during the Battle of Chancellorsville.

Location: 36382 Constitution Hwy., Locust Grove, Virginia 22508

Ellwood.

Walk the Clearing at Saunders Field
Fredericksburg and Spotsylvania National Military Park, Virginia

Why? *The struggle for Saunders Field at the Wilderness marked the beginning of one of the longest and most savage periods of combat in American history.*

Description: On May 4, 1864, the Union Army of the Potomac crossed the Rapidan River to begin what would be known as the Overland Campaign, the longest and bloodiest period of sustained fighting in American history up to that point. General Ulysses S. Grant, in overall command of the Federals, was leading an army in combat in Virginia for the first time. Lurking in the woods a few miles away were elements of the Army of Northern Virginia under Robert E. Lee.

Fortifications near the edge of Saunders Field.

About midday on May 5, the Union V Corps under General Gouverneur Warren encountered elements of Confederate General Richard Ewell's Second Corps. Ordered to "pitch in," Warren's 12,000 men attacked the Confederates entrenched on the western edge of Saunders Field, one of the few clearings in the Wilderness. A "wild, wicked roar" of musketry engulfed the Union lines and soon a brutal and savage round of hand-to-hand combat took place. Eventually, the unsupported Union troops were compelled to retreat back across Saunders Field, in the open and extremely vulnerable to enemy fire. The battle was fought elsewhere for the remainder of the day and into the next. However, just as the sun began to set on May 6, as the Federals were fixing their dinners, chaos broke. Five thousand Confederates under General John Gordon stormed the Union right flank, scattering blue-coated soldiers and nabbing more than eight hundred prisoners, including two generals. Saunders Field was again turned into a scene of savage combat. Eventually, darkness and a stiffening defense enabled the Union army to re-establish its lines. Gordon later wrote, "The greatest opportunity ever presented to Lee's army was permitted to pass."

Today, the National Park Service maintains an exhibit shelter and walking trails at Saunders Field. Make sure you visit the battlefield sites, including the Widow Tapp Farm.

Location: 35510 Constitution Hwy., Locust Grove, Virginia 22508

Tour the Mine Run Battlefield at Payne's Farm
Locust Grove, Virginia

Why? *This is a splendid opportunity to see a well-preserved battlefield and learn about a little-known battle fought on November 27, 1863.*

Description: Payne's Farm was the scene of the heaviest fighting during the often overlooked Mine Run Campaign. In November 1863, General George Gordon Meade, commander of the Army of the Potomac, attempted to steal a march on General Robert E. Lee and his Army of Northern Virginia by slipping across the Rapidan River to attack Lee's right flank. General Jubal A. Early, in temporary command of the Confederate Second Corps, marched east on the Orange Turnpike to meet General William French's slow-moving Union III Corps near Payne's Farm. French, whose qualifications for command of an army corps were dubious at best, should have already been united with other elements of the Union army. But his dilatoriness enabled the aggressive Early to catch the III Corps, on November 27, isolated without ready support.

The heaviest fighting of the Mine Run Campaign occurred here, at Payne's Farm.

The result was desperate fighting on Payne's Farm that pitted French's men against the outnumbered men of Stonewall Jackson's former division (now commanded by General Edward "Allegheny" Johnson). After dark, Lee withdrew his army to prepared field entrenchments along the steep slopes of a nearby creek called Mine Run. Skirmishing along Mine Run occurred for several days, but Meade wisely determined that the Confederate line was simply too strong to risk an attack and ultimately retreated during the night of December 1–2, thus ending his last campaign of 1863. The Payne's Farm fighting set the stage for the Battle of the Wilderness five months later in May of 1864.

Location: 31334 Zoar Rd., Locust Grove, Virginia 22508

Experience the Bloody Angle at Spotsylvania
Fredericksburg and Spotsylvania National Military Park, Virginia

Why? Some of the most desperate American fighting unfolded on this spot.

Description: Following the Battle of the Wilderness, the armies of Generals Robert E. Lee and Ulysses S. Grant raced for the strategic crossroads at Spotsylvania Court House. If Grant had won the race, he would be between the Confederate army and Richmond. By the narrowest of margins, however, Lee's army won. The Southerners quickly dug entrenchments to defend against the expected attack.

A slight angle in the freshly dug entrenchments caught Grant's eye. He sensed it was a vulnerable point in the Confederate lines, and he launched two attacks against it. The first, a minor attack by 5,000 men under Colonel Emory Upton, succeeded in briefly breaking the Rebel

An early postwar view of the Bloody Angle.

lines. The second, on May 12, 1864, was on a much larger scale and succeeded handsomely, at first. Union troops captured 3,000 of Lee's soldiers, two generals, and twenty cannons. Lee quickly counterattacked, however, and for the next twenty hours the two sides engaged in brutal and savage combat in a driving rain storm. Bodies piled up three, four, and even five deep in the mud. But the fighting bought Lee the time he needed to build a new line of entrenchments. When his men retreated to the new line, they left behind a landscape of unspeakable horror.

The Spotsylvania Battlefield has much more to it than just the Bloody Angle. Take the National Park Service driving tour, walk around the McCoull House, see the place where General "Uncle John" Sedgwick was killed, and check out the historic courthouse itself.

Location: Grant Drive, Spotsylvania, Virginia 22553

Confederate fortifications at Spotsylvania.

Stand in Grant's Footsteps at Massaponax
Massaponax, Virginia

Why? *Stand where the Federal high command was photographed after the Battle of Spotsylvania.*

Description: After two weeks of heavy fighting at Spotsylvania Court House, on May 21, 1864, Union Generals Ulysses S. Grant and George G. Meade reached Massaponax Church on the strategic Telegraph Road. After a short conference, the two generals and the army continued southward toward Guinea Station, in an attempt to get around Lee's army. Photographer Timothy O'Sullivan ascended the church stairs, pointed his bulky camera out the second-story window, and captured three incredible photographs of the generals and their staffs in conference, sitting on pews. The photos were taken from the window above and to the right of the main entrance, and they show wagons on the Massaponax Church Road in the background. Preserved soldier graffiti still covers the upper walls inside the church.

Location: 5101 Massaponax Church Rd., Massaponax, Virginia 22407

Ulysses S. Grant and his staff outside the church with army wagons passing in a blur behind.

LEARN ABOUT LEE'S TRAP AT NORTH ANNA
North Anna Battlefield, Virginia

Why? *The battle of North Anna nearly transformed the war in Virginia. Lee's tactical gamble briefly left Grant's army divided and vulnerable to be destroyed in pieces.*

Description: After the battle of Spotsylvania Court House, the exhausted armies marched toward the North Anna River. Lee's army reached the stream crossings first and built extensive earthworks on the south side of the river. His lines took the shape of an inverted "V," with the apex anchored at Ox Ford on the North Anna. This unusual arrangement forced the Union army to divide while crossing the river—each part unable to quickly come to the assistance of another.

Union soldiers in trenches near Chesterfield Bridge above the North Anna River.

Not realizing that Lee had outmaneuvered him, Grant divided his army. Unfortunately for the Confederates, however, Lee fell ill at this time and was unable to take advantage of what proved to be his last great opportunity to destroy an isolated part of the Federal army. Unable to exert personal control over the army, he had to leave the plan in the hands of cautious subordinates who failed to launch a concentrated attack against the divided Yankees. Following General A. P. Hill's failed attack at Jericho Mills on the Union right flank, Lee exclaimed in frustration, "Why did you not do as Jackson would have done, thrown your whole force upon those people and driven them back?" Belatedly, Grant would realize his perilous position, and withdrew both wings of the army back across the North Anna River. Eventually, both armies continued moving south.

Today, Hanover County maintains a 2.4-mile interpretive trail that guides visitors around some of the most pristine earthworks and rifle pits in existence.

Location: 12075 Verdon Rd., Doswell, Virginia 23047

STAND IN THE MIDDLE FIELD AT THIRD WINCHESTER
Third Winchester Battlefield, Virginia

Why? The bloodiest field in the bloodiest battle in the Shenandoah Valley, once slated to become a residential housing development, is now complete with trails and lively interpretive signage.

Description: The Third Battle of Winchester has the dubious honor of being the bloodiest battle fought in the Shenandoah Valley. On September 19, 1864, Union General Philip Sheridan's 39,000-man army attacked the Confederate Army of the Valley under General Jubal Early. Despite

The Middle Field—the bloodiest field in the Shenandoah Valley.

being outnumbered nearly three to one, Early's veterans put up a stubborn defense. Early was able to delay the advance of the Union VI and XIX Corps long enough to concentrate his army. The bloodiest fighting of the battle occurred in what came to be known as the Middle Field, located between two distinct woodlots that marked the approximate positions of the opposing armies. Here, the outnumbered Confederates launched a counterattack on a particularly vulnerable part of the Union line. The intensity of the fighting and artillery battle led one Union commander to exclaim, "My God! . . . This is a perfect slaughterhouse." Despite Early's brief success in the Middle Field, Sheridan was able to call on his reserves. The odds against the Confederates became overwhelming, and Early's army melted away under the pressure. Many soldiers were caught fleeing the battlefield in panic.

The Civil War Trust's walking trail will take you along Hackwood Lane, through the Middle Field, and to the famous woodlots of the battle.

Location: 106 Great Pond Way, Winchester, Virginia 22603

TOUR BELLE GROVE AND CEDAR CREEK BATTLEFIELD
Belle Grove and Cedar Creek National Historic Park, Virginia

Why? Historic Belle Grove plantation was at the epicenter of fighting during the 1864 battle of Cedar Creek.

Description: Belle Grove Plantation, constructed in the 1790s of native limestone still mined in the area, is one of the most famous manor houses

Civil War veterans at Belle Grove.

of the Shenandoah Valley. At one time, it was the center of a 7,500-acre plantation that employed more than one hundred slaves. Belle Grove is, however, best known for its role in the battle of Cedar Creek, one of the most decisive encounters of the Civil War. Fought on October 19, 1864, it pitted two of the most colorful characters of the war against one another—dour Confederate General Jubal A. Early versus the energetic cavalryman General Phil Sheridan. In the morning, Early's surprise attack on the Union army roared past Belle Grove, and threatened to inflict an embarrassing defeat on the much larger Federal army. In the afternoon, a Union counterattack led by Sheridan crushed Early's army and forever ended Confederate control of the Valley. At Belle Grove, you can learn more about this pivotal battle, see the parlor that Sheridan used as his headquarters, and stand in the nursery where Confederate General Stephen Ramseur died from wounds received during the battle.

Take the time to stand on the porch and gaze at the Massanutten Mountain. Although threatened by mining operations in the closest proximity to the scene of the fight, much of the battlefield surrounding the manor is in a solid state of preservation. An interpretive center on US Route 11 provides additional information. Check the National Park Service's website for information on upcoming programs at Cedar Creek.

Location: 336 Belle Grove Rd., Middletown, Virginia 22645

SEE THE FIELD OF LOST SHOES AT NEW MARKET
New Market Battlefield State Historical Park, Virginia

Why? *Across this field the teenaged cadets of the Virginia Military Institute (VMI) charged like veterans against a line of massed Union artillery. They captured a Union gun while suffering 20 percent casualties.*

Description: As part of his spring 1864 Union offensive, General Ulysses S. Grant ordered General Franz Sigel to advance against the small Rebel army defending the Valley. Sigel's mission was to prevent the Confederates, under the command of General John Breckinridge, from reinforcing General Robert E. Lee's army in central Virginia. However, Sigel's snail-like advance up the Valley gave Breckinridge the time he needed to muster additional soldiers for his Valley Army, including local militia and the 257-strong corps of cadets from VMI.

On May 15, 1864, outside the small Valley Pike town of New Market, the two antagonists finally met. Breckinridge drew first blood, launching an attack that liberated New Market and drove the Unionists back to a hill overlooking the Bushong Farm. Eventually, Breckinridge ordered an advance against the new Union line, bristling with Yankee cannon. Needing every available man in line, he reluctantly said, "Put the boys in." The cadets advanced against the Union line, many of them losing their shoes in a muddy gully, which would be known thereafter as the "Field of Lost Shoes." The charge was a success, and Sigel was forced to flee across the north fork of the Shenandoah River. Today, the cadets' immortal charge is memorialized in the Hall of Valor Museum, located a short distance from where they met the test of battle.

Location: 8895 George Collins Parkway, New Market, Virginia 22844

The Bushong House at New Market.

Understand Jackson's Brilliance at Port Republic
Port Republic, Virginia

Why? *Port Republic was the final battle of Stonewall Jackson's Valley campaign, a campaign that made Jackson a legend.*

Description: The Battle of Port Republic, fought June 9, 1862, was the final clash of Stonewall Jackson's famous Shenandoah Valley Campaign. Jackson, confronted by two separate Union forces, defeated the first one on June 8 at the Battle of Cross Keys. This victory enabled him to concentrate his forces against the isolated division of General James Shields, advancing south through the Luray Valley.

The battle began with the advance of Jackson's beloved Stonewall Brigade across the Lewis Farm. His Virginians came under heavy fire, and were repulsed with significant losses. Meanwhile, the brigade's reinforcements (a division under General Richard Ewell) were delayed by the partial collapse of a makeshift bridge across the south fork of the Shenandoah River. Eventually, Ewell was able to launch an attack on the Coaling, a key Union artillery position just south of the Lewis farmstead (and site of previous charcoal production). After repeated attacks, Ewell's men captured the Coaling, unhinging the Union line. Shields had little choice but to retreat northward. The twin victories at Cross Keys and Port Republic marked the climax of Jackson's campaign, and freed him to reinforce General Robert E. Lee's army during the Seven Days' Battles east of Richmond.

Location: 7114 Ore Rd., Port Republic, Virginia 24471

CLIMB SITLINGTON'S HILL AT MCDOWELL
McDowell, Virginia

Why? *McDowell was arguably one of Stonewall Jackson's most important victories and set the stage for his renowned 1862 Valley Campaign. Climb the hill to see how and where he did it.*

Description: In early May 1862, General Stonewall Jackson was pondering the best method for defeating the Federal armies slowly converging on his small force. He decided to attack the army of Union General John C. Fremont, which was slowly advancing into the Valley from western Virginia. The defeat of Fremont would free Jackson to thrust northward against the other Union forces threatening the Valley. Reinforced by General Edward "Allegheny" Johnson's division, Jackson confronted Fremont's army at McDowell on May 8. It was actually the Union army that began the battle, launching an attack on Jackson's men arrayed at the top of picturesque Sitlington's Hill, near modern Route 250. After four hours of heavy fighting, the Federals were repulsed, leaving dead and wounded sprawled along the slopes of the hill. Fremont's men subsequently retreated back into western Virginia, exactly as Jackson had hoped.

Climbing up Sitlington Hill along the interpretive trail enables you to get a better understanding of the difficulties confronting the Union soldiers, who fought the battle after an exhausting climb up the hill. Sitlington Hill is among the best preserved of the Valley battlefield sites. The Felix Hull House, Jackson's headquarters after the battle, still stands.

Location: 161 Mansion House Rd., McDowell, Virginia 24458

Civil War Trust signage atop Sitlington's Hill—a site well worth the difficult climb.

Visit Robert E. Lee's Office and Tomb
Washington and Lee University, Lexington, Virginia

Why? Robert E. Lee lived and worked here in the last four years of his life, and he was buried here upon his death.

Description: Following his surrender at Appomattox, Lee was eager to find a quiet place where he could work and support his family. He succeeded in his quest when he arrived at Washington College in Lexington, Virginia (now known as Washington and Lee University). Lee served as the school's president from 1865 until his death in October 1870. During his presidency, he oversaw the construction of a college chapel. The Victorian design probably is the work of Lee's son, George Washington Custis Lee, with some help from Colonel Thomas Williamson. Upon Lee's death, he was buried in a crypt beneath the chapel. Today, the crypt also holds members of Lee's family, including his wife, Mary, his seven children, and his parents. The chapel boasts the famous "Recumbent Lee" statue designed by Edward Valentine. The basement is home to a museum that tells the story of the George Washington and Lee families. It is also the location of Lee's office, which has been painstakingly preserved in almost exactly the same condition it was when Lee left it for the last time. Lee's famous warhorse, Traveller, is buried outside the Chapel.

Location: Washington and Lee University, Lexington, Virginia 24450

The tomb of Robert E. Lee.

SEE STONEWALL JACKSON'S HORSE
Virginia Military Institute, Lexington, Virginia

Why? *The VMI Museum is a treasure trove of Civil War history that stresses the role of VMI in the conflict as well as the career of Stonewall Jackson.*

Description: The Virginia Military Institute (VMI) Museum traces its origins to 1856, when its superintendent accepted a Revolutionary War musket for display at the institute. It is considered the first public museum in Virginia. Today, the museum collects, preserves, interprets, and displays the heritage of VMI through its unparalleled 15,000-artifact collection. The museum's Civil War collection, particularly its mementos of Confederate General Thomas "Stonewall" Jackson, is extensive. It has Jackson's favorite hat, several of Jackson's uniforms (including that which he was wearing when he was wounded at Chancellorsville), and items from his days as a VMI professor. The most unusual object must be the mounted hide of his war horse, Little Sorrel, who carried him through many of his battles in the Shenandoah Valley. VMI is often referred to as the "West Point of the South," and the museum emphasizes the role of the Institute's 1,700 alumni who served in the Confederate Army throughout the course of the war. This includes several artifacts of the Battle of New Market, where the VMI Corps of Cadets fought with exceptional gallantry on May 15, 1864. Six cadets killed during this battle are buried on the VMI grounds.

Location: 415 Letcher Ave., Lexington, Virginia 24450

GO IN AND ON FORT MONROE
Fort Monroe, Virginia

Why? *Although never attacked, Fort Monroe was a sanctuary for slaves fleeing the South and was where Confederate President Jefferson Davis was imprisoned after the war.*

Description: One of the largest masonry forts in America, Fort Monroe was a major Federal stronghold throughout the Civil War. Located in the heart of strategic Hampton Roads, it was reinforced to provide the Union army with a vital base within striking distance of Norfolk, Yorktown, and even Richmond. With help from the Navy, soldiers from Fort Monroe extended Federal control along the coasts of the Carolinas. Several land operations were also launched from the fort, including the battle of Big Bethel in June 1861, General George McClellan's Peninsula Campaign of 1862, and the siege of Suffolk in 1863. In the early days of the war, Union General Benjamin Butler, who was commanding the fort, issued his famous "contraband" order declaring that slaves who escaped and reached Union lines would not be returned to bondage. As a result, Fort Monroe became a sanctuary for escaped slaves throughout the conflict. After the war, Confederate President Jefferson Davis was imprisoned here from 1865–1867, and his prison cell is the main attraction in the fort's Casemate Museum.

Location: 20 Bernard Rd., Fort Monroe, Virginia 23651

The "Lincoln Gun" at Fort Monroe.

HERITAGE AREAS

Although numerous heritage areas are scattered across the United States, several pertain to the Civil War in particular, including the Tennessee Civil War National Heritage Area, Virginia's Mosby Heritage Area and Shenandoah Valley Battlefield National Historical District, Maryland's Heart of the Civil War Heritage Area, the Journey Through Hallowed Ground National Heritage Area stretching from Virginia to Pennsylvania, and Freedom's Frontier National Heritage Area in Kansas.

Each one of these heritage areas strives to tell the story of the Civil War, freedom, emancipation, and Reconstruction by highlighting the battlefields themselves, as well as the vast array of homes, neighborhoods, and towns significantly impacted by the Civil War. Some heritage areas are vast in their footprint—the Tennessee Civil War National Heritage Area encompasses the entire Volunteer State, offering numerous driving tours, museums, and other attractions. The Journey Through Hallowed Ground is a treasure trove of sites illustrating the early centuries of American history. Follow the Old Carolina Road (Rt. 15/231) from founding father Thomas Jefferson's home at Monticello, in Albemarle County, Virginia, to the great battlefield at Gettysburg, Pennsylvania, and you will encounter Native American and African American sites, restored architectural gems, presidential homes, and the greatest concentration of Civil War battlefields anywhere.

More regionally, Virginia's Mosby Heritage Area covers some 1,800 square miles of Northern Virginia, west of Washington, D.C. Elsewhere in the Old Dominion, the Shenandoah Valley became a major theater of the war, due to its strategic location settled between the Bull Run and Blue Ridge Mountains to the east and west, and the Potomac and Rappahannock Rivers to the north and south. In Maryland, the Heart of the Civil War Heritage Area stretches across Frederick, Washington, and Carroll Counties, featuring sites associated with two of the Civil War's bloodiest military campaigns, Antietam and Gettysburg, as well as Monocacy, the "battle that saved Washington."

See the *Monitor*'s Turret at the Mariners' Museum
Newport News, Virginia

Why? *See the original turret of the* Monitor, *one of the most famous warships of all time. You can also walk upon a replica of this early ironclad vessel's deck.*

Description: Finished in 1862, the USS *Monitor* was the first ironclad built for the U.S. Navy. The *Monitor* is best known for her participation in the first naval battle between two ironclad warships, fought in Hampton Roads in early March 1862. On March 8, the first Confederate ironclad, the CSS *Virginia*, built from the hull of the USS *Merrimac*, wreaked havoc on the wooden vessels of the Union fleet anchored in Hampton Roads. The next day, the *Virginia* returned to finish its bloody work, when confronted by the *Monitor*. The result was an hours-long battle, in which the two ironclads fought to a draw. The *Monitor* is also noted for several important naval innovations, most notably the rotating turret, which spurred a "revolution" in shipbuilding. The Mariners' Museum's USS *Monitor* Center contains priceless relics of the famous warship, including her turret, propeller, anchor, engine, and many personal effects of crew members. Upon arriving at the museum, these artifacts were stored in special tanks for several years to stabilize the metal. Most recovered items are now on public display, along with a full-scale replica of the *Monitor* deck and part of the *Virginia* as well.

Location: 100 Museum Dr., Newport News, Virginia 23606

The deck and turret of the USS *Monitor*.

Tour the Confederate White House
Richmond, Virginia

Why? *The Confederate White House served as the home and office of President Jefferson Davis during nearly the entire war. Next door is the unrivaled collection of artifacts maintained by the Museum of the Confederacy.*

Description: The Confederate White House and Museum of the Confederacy are among the premiere Civil War attractions in Richmond. Restored to its wartime appearance, the mansion was the scene of cabinet meetings and some of the most important decisions of the war. Robert E. Lee frequently met with Davis in the house.

The White House of the Confederacy, 1865.

The Museum of the Confederacy, located across the courtyard from the White House, is the repository of the world's most comprehensive collection of Confederate artifacts, including flags, photos, documents, and many personal effects of generals and common soldiers alike. Among the relics are uniforms, sidearms, and other items owned by Jefferson Davis, Robert E. Lee, Joseph E. Johnston, John Bell Hood, Stonewall Jackson, J. E. B. Stuart, Wade Hampton, Raphael Semmes, and others. Among the museum's most popular items is its collection of more than 500 original wartime battle flags carried by the various Confederate armies. Many were donated by war veterans in the museum's early years, while numerous regimental flags captured during the war were transferred from the U.S. War Department. Check the museum's website for any changes to locations and hours.

Location: 1201 East Clay St., Richmond, Virginia 23219

Visit the Confederate Arsenal at Tredegar
Richmond, Virginia

Why? *Tredegar was once the most important iron foundry in the South. Today, it serves as the visitor center for Richmond National Battlefield.*

Description: Any tour of Civil War Richmond should include a stop at the Tredegar Iron Works. At the start of the Civil War, Tredegar was the South's only rolling mill capable of producing cannon and armor plating for iron-clad naval vessels. It is estimated that half of all the cannons produced in the Confederate States were forged at Tredegar.

Today, the once sprawling iron foundry now serves as the main visitor center for the Richmond National Battlefield Park. Exhibits interpret Civil War Richmond and its role as the capital of the Confederacy. Visitors are encouraged to see some of the sites associated with the National Park, including Chimborazo Hospital, the Seven Days' battlefields, and Cold Harbor. Tredegar is also home of the American Civil War Center at Historic Tredegar, a private museum that tells the story of the Civil War from three different perspectives: Union, Confederate, and African American. The center contains interactive theaters, plasma-screen maps, artifacts, and more to tell the story of the Civil War. Tredegar is also an excellent jumping off point for walking tours of Civil War sites around the city, including the nearby Belle Isle prison site, just across a somewhat harrowing pedestrian bridge.

Location: 470 Tredegar St., Richmond, Virginia 23219

Tredegar Iron
Works, 1865.

SEE THE BLOODIEST OF THE SEVEN DAYS: GAINES' MILL
Richmond National Battlefield Park, Virginia

Why? At Gaines' Mill, the attacking Confederates paid a terrible price in blood to drive the Union invader away from the capital at Richmond.

Description: The Seven Days' Battles, fought in the early summer of 1862, witnessed the emergence of General Robert E. Lee as a great commander and lifted the Union threat to Richmond. Lee's army, recently christened the Army of Northern Virginia, was not yet the efficient military machine it would become, and the Seven Days' Battles were characterized by uncoordinated attacks and missed opportunities. The third and bloodiest battle of the campaign, Gaines' Mill, was no exception.

After the battle of Mechanicsville on June 26, the Union V Corps under General Fitz John Porter withdrew to defensive positions behind

Battlefield remains at Gaines' Mill.

Boatswain's Swamp near Gaines' Mill. Porter was ordered by his commander, General George McClellan, to hold his position "at all costs." For most of the day Porter did just that, holding firm against disjointed, mismanaged attacks, inflicting heavy casualties in the process. As dusk approached, the Confederates finally launched a coordinated attack, led by General John Bell Hood's hardbitten Texas Brigade. This attack broke Porter's line and drove his men back toward the river, but the exhausted Confederates were too disorganized to pursue the fleeing Union soldiers. That night, the Federals retreated back across the Chickahominy River to safety. More than 15,000 were killed, wounded, or captured. Richmond National Battlefield Park currently owns sixty acres of this battlefield, including the spot where Hood's Confederates finally managed to break through the Union line.

Location: 6283 Watt House Rd., Mechanicsville, Virginia 23111

TOUR GLENDALE AND MALVERN HILL
Richmond National Battlefield, Virginia

Why? *Glendale and Malvern Hill, two of the most decisive battles of the 1862 Seven Days' campaign, are also the best preserved. The dramatic views from the Union lines on Malvern Hill are breathtaking.*

Description: On June 30, 1862, the Confederate divisions of Generals Benjamin Huger, James Longstreet, and A. P. Hill converged on elements of the retreating Federals at Glendale in an attempt to block the Union line of retreat and more. The attacks of Longstreet and Hill broke the Federal defenses near Willis Church, in the process destroying General George McCall's division, one of the finest units in the Northern army. However, violent Union counterattacks led by Generals Joseph Hooker and Phil Kearny resulted in some of the most terrific fighting of the war to date. By the time darkness settled in, the Union line had been stabilized and the Federal army was able to retreat along the Willis Church Road. The Union army suffered some 3,800 casualties, while the Confederates suffered 3,600 casualties. General Robert E. Lee's best chance to trap and destroy the Army of the Potomac before it got back to its James River defenses had been lost.

The gentle slope of Malvern Hill does little to tell the story of an artillery hell in 1862.

The next day, the united Union army confronted the Confederates from a strong defensive position on Malvern Hill. Despite the strength of the position, Lee was unwilling to let the Federals get away without one more push. In a desperate attempt to attack General McClellan's army before it got back to its impenetrable James River defenses, the Confederates launched a series of badly mismanaged and disjointed attacks against the massed Northern artillery on Malvern Hill. As a result, Lee's army suffered over 5,300 needless casualties. Despite this lopsided victory, McClellan continued his withdrawal to Harrison's Landing, where his army would be protected by Union gunboats. This battle was the final clash of McClellan's ill-fated Peninsula Campaign.

Location: 8301 Willis Church Rd., Henrico, Virginia 23231
9175 Willis Church Rd., Henrico, Virginia 23231

PRESERVATION

"In great deeds something abides. On great fields something
stays. Forms change and pass; bodies disappear; but spirits
linger, to consecrate ground for the vision-place of souls.

And reverent men and women from afar, and generations
that know us not and that we know not of, heart-drawn to see
where and by whom great things were suffered and done for
them, shall come to this deathless field to ponder and dream;
and lo! The shadow of a mighty presence shall wrap them in
its bosom, and the power of the vision pass into their souls."

Joshua Lawrence Chamberlain, October 3, 1889

More than two decades after fighting in the bloody battle of Gettysburg,
Joshua Lawrence Chamberlain made this statement during a dedication
ceremony for the monument of the 20th Maine Volunteers, the unit he commanded during the great battle. His words illustrate the transporting power of
Civil War battlefields. Today, at Gettysburg, one can still return to that same
"deathless field to ponder and dream," but the same cannot be said of all Civil
War battlefields; even at some legendary locations, the experience can only
be as strong as your imagination, since you have to picture a field where now
stands a mall, or block out the sound of trucks roaring past on nearby highways.

Certain moments are suspended within the consciousness of all Americans. Those born in the first part of the 20th century will never forget the Great
Depression or WWII, while the trauma of the Kennedy assassination and Viet-
nam War are indelible memories for Baby Boomers. For younger generations,
the terrorist attacks of September 11, 2001, and subsequent military engagements are a similarly defining moment in history.

Although we can argue over whether or not a particular military action was
justified, we can agree that war is sometimes necessary to defend and preserve
our way of life. And as the philosopher George Santayana once intoned, if we
are unable to remember and learn from the lessons of our past, even its darker

elements, we are destined to repeat it. Historic preservation is the duty of all Americans, as we stand in awe of those who fought, many giving, as President Lincoln said, the "last full measure of devotion." And while reading books about these brave souls may be inspirational, it is no substitute for visiting the actual places where these epic struggles took place.

Unfortunately, our Civil War battlefields are rapidly disappearing, with approximately thirty acres paved over each day. But this can change; planned development and historic preservation can go hand in hand, when civic duty and patriotism are given precedence over greed and personal gain.

Today, it's more important than ever to protect this hallowed ground where the future of our nation was shaped, because time is running out to preserve battlefields near major urban centers. To learn how you can help protect these irreplaceable landscapes for future generations, visit the Civil War Trust's website at www.civilwar.org.

CONTEMPLATE CONFEDERATE TRENCHES AT COLD HARBOR
Richmond National Battlefield Park, Virginia

Why? *Walk this battlefield and you may experience a taste of the dread and terror that Union soldiers felt as they advanced on the maze of Confederate earthworks.*

Description: At the end of May 1864, after a month of sustained fighting that began in the Wilderness, Grant's and Lee's armies had reached the outskirts of Richmond. On May 31, Union and Confederate horsemen engaged in a race for the crossroads of Old Cold Harbor—a race won by the blue-coated troopers. Attempts by Southern infantry to dislodge the Federal cavalry on June 1 proved futile and Lee's army dug in. Union attacks on the outnumbered Rebels during the first three days of June were equally unsuccessful, resulting in extremely high casualties among

Cold Harbor's fortifications were made of earth as well as everything else the soldiers could find.

the Union attackers. Indeed, the odds were so long that many Union soldiers pinned their names to their uniforms so their bodies could be identified after the battle. Grant later wrote, "I have always regretted that the last assault at Cold Harbor was ever made. . . . At Cold Harbor no advantage whatever was gained to compensate for the heavy loss we sustained." For the next nine days, the armies confronted one another in their trenches, sometimes only yards apart. Soldiers on both sides were tormented by the pitiful cries of the wounded and the putrefying smell of the dead, still lying between the lines in "no man's land." On June 12, Grant moved south toward additional battles south of the James River. Look at the electric map at the Cold Harbor Battlefield Visitor Center and walk the self-guided, one-mile trail that begins behind the building.

Location: 5515 Anderson-Wright Dr., Mechanicsville, Virginia 23111

SEE THE DOMINANCE OF DREWRY'S BLUFF
Richmond, Virginia

Why? *The well-preserved Confederate fortifications here saved Richmond from a daring naval attack in May 1862 and again in 1864. Drewry's Bluff offers a beautiful view of the James River.*

Description: After the fall of Yorktown in early May 1862, the Confederate army evacuated Norfolk and scuttled the ironclad Virginia. The James River became an obvious avenue for Union advance on Richmond. The incomplete Confederate defenses at Drewry's Bluff, eight miles below Richmond at a bend in the river, were all that stood between the heart of the Confederate capital and the Union Navy. These earthen defenses, known to the Federals as Fort Darling, were commanded by Confederate Com-

Confederate artillery completely dominated the James River at Drewry's Bluff.

mander Ebenezer Farrand. On May 15, 1862, five Union gunboats of the James River Flotilla, including the ironclads *Monitor* and *Galena*, steamed up the James to attack Richmond. At Drewry's Bluff they encountered man-made obstacles in the river and accurate fire from the artillery batteries at Fort Darling. Although the shells did little to damage the *Monitor*, the ironclad could not return fire effectively because its crew could not elevate the barrels on the ship's guns high enough to hit the battery on the bluff. The *Galena* took more than forty hits throughout the four-hour battle and was severely damaged. Meanwhile, Confederate sharpshooters posted along the banks targeted the sailors and even wounded one of the ship's captains. Under such intense fire, the Union flotilla had no choice but to abandon its attack on Richmond. Two years later, Union General Benjamin Butler tried but failed to capture the fort.

Drewry's Bluff is somewhat difficult to find but is well worth the detour and the pleasant walk on the National Park Service trail.

Location: 7600 Fort Darling Rd., Richmond, Virginia 23237

Take the Trevilian Station Driving Tour
Louisa, Virginia

Why? *This often-overlooked cavalry battle, fought on June 11–12, 1864, has been called George Armstrong Custer's "first last stand."*

Description: While the main bodies of General Robert E. Lee's and General Ulysses S. Grant's armies were fighting at Cold Harbor, near Richmond, Philip Sheridan's Federal cavalry rode west to disrupt communication and supply lines into and out of the Confederate capital, with Southern horsemen in hot pursuit. These forces clashed for two days at Trevilian Station, on the Virginia Central Railroad near the Louisa Courthouse. Although the Confederate cavalry was able to stop the raid, their absence from the main front allowed Grant's army to slip across the James River to Petersburg. Your multi-stop driving tour of the Trevilian Station battlefield, courtesy of the Trevilian Station Battlefield Foundation, begins at the Louisa Courthouse.

Location: 180 West Main St., Louisa, Virginia 23093

Trevilian Station.

EXPERIENCE THE REAL WIDTH OF THE JAMES RIVER
Wilcox's Landing, Charles City, Virginia

Why? *The only way to truly grasp the extraordinary military obstacle of the James River is to stand upon its banks and gaze across. And crossing the James was a major step toward ending the Civil War in Virginia.*

Description: After more than a month of bloodshed that began with two days of fighting at the Wilderness, Grant's army was stalled at Cold Harbor. Realizing that he had run out of options north of the James River, Grant made the decision to move south to the Confederate railroad hub at Petersburg. The march began at dark on June 12, 1864, with a twenty-mile march to the James. From June 14 through June 17—here at Wilcox's Landing and three miles downstream at Weyanoke Point—the Army of the Potomac did the impossible: crossed the river on thousands of feet of primitive pontoon bridges, accompanied by thousands of supply wagons. Despite the complicated maneuver, Grant was able to keep the crossing a secret. It proved to be one of only a few times during the entire war that anybody had successfully managed to outmaneuver General Robert E. Lee.

Location: 12654 Wilcox Wharf Rd., Charles City, Virginia 23030

Tour the Manor and Wharves at City Point
Petersburg National Battlefield, City Point Unit, Virginia

Why? *The sleepy river community of City Point was the Union army headquarters during the siege of Petersburg. Its wharves overflowed with food and supplies for the Northern armies.*

Description: In June 1864, as the exhausted armies settled down to a siege of Petersburg, General Ulysses S. Grant established his headquarters at City Point, Virginia. Grant's headquarters tents were located on the grounds of Appomattox Manor. Later, when it became clear the siege would be of long duration, cabins were built for Grant and his staff. You can still see Grant's cabin, reconstructed using some of the original materials, as well as tour the interior of the manor house.

City Point's location at the confluence of the James and Appomattox Rivers, coupled with its proximity to rail lines, made it a strategic position of the first order. City Point rapidly became one of the busiest ports in the South as countless ships brought tons of supplies to the Union army. On a typical day, the Union army had nine million meals and 12,000 tons of hay and oats stored at City Point. The on-site bakery could produce 100,000 rations of bread per day. Eventually, the U.S. Military Railroad construction corps extended the railroad at City Point west and south behind the lengthy Union siege lines.

Location: 1001 Pecan Ave., Hopewell, Virginia 23860

Images like these show City Point's status as one of the world's busiest ports—for a time.

Tour the Battlefields of Bermuda Hundred
Prince George, Virginia

Why? *Bermuda Hundred was the scene of an overlooked and ultimately unsuccessful campaign against Richmond's supply lines in the spring of 1864.*

Description: General Ulysses S. Grant's goal for the 1864 spring campaign was to have all Union armies, large and small, advance at the same time and put unbearable pressure on the outnumbered Confederates. Part of that plan included an advance on the vital supply lines into Richmond by the Union Army of the James, while Grant had General Robert E. Lee occupied north of the Confederate capital. Unfortunately for Grant, the Army of the James was commanded by Benjamin Butler, a political general with few military skills. When Butler disembarked his army of more than

Fort Harrison, one of many Bermuda Hundred–area sites, is preserved by the National Park Service.

30,000 soldiers at Bermuda Hundred, he confronted a rag-tag "army" of teenagers and old men patched together by Confederate General P. G. T. Beauregard. Beauregard's men should have been no match for Butler's. After a series of battles, however, Beauregard was able to "bottle up" Butler in the Bermuda Hundred peninsula, preventing any further attack on Richmond's supply lines. So well had Butler been thwarted that Beauregard was able to send reinforcements to Lee in time for the fighting at Cold Harbor. A self-guided tour of the Bermuda Hundred battlefields is available at both Richmond National Battlefield and Petersburg National Battlefield. Extensive earthworks and fortifications are still visible.

Location: Chesterfield County, Virginia 23875

GAZE INTO THE CRATER
Petersburg National Battlefield, Virginia

Why? *You will explore a battlefield where one of the most extraordinary events of the Civil War took place.*

Description: Although exhausted from the intense fighting of previous months, the armies confronting one another in the trench lines at Petersburg were not satisfied with stalemate. Colonel Henry Pleasants, whose 48th Pennsylvania regiment was recruited in the state's coal mining region, proposed digging a mine under the Confederate lines. The suggestion was favorably received by his corps commander, General Ambrose Burnside. From June 25 until July 27, 1864, Pleasants' regiment dug forty to fifty feet per day, excavating 18,000 cubic feet of earth by hand with simple picks and shovels. The entire tunnel stretched some 510 feet long, ending beneath the Confederate lines. The regiment then packed the tunnel with 320 kegs of black powder explosive. Early on July 30, the Federals exploded the mine beneath Pegram's Salient, blowing an immense gap in the Confederate defenses at Petersburg. From this

A view of the Crater, looking toward the Union position.

propitious beginning, everything deteriorated rapidly for the Union attackers. Unit after unit charged into and around the crater, where soldiers milled about in confusion. Among them was a division of black soldiers who had been especially trained for the assault but, because of prejudice, was not permitted to lead it. The Confederates quickly recovered and launched counterattacks that ultimately sealed the break in their lines. The Federals were repulsed with horrendous casualties. Burnside was relieved of command for his role in the debacle. No wonder General Grant referred to this moment as "the saddest affair I have witnessed in the war."

Location: 5001 Siege Rd., Petersburg, Virginia 23803

Visit Blandford Church and Cemetery
Petersburg, Virginia

Why? The Blandford Church Cemetery is the final resting place of 30,000 Confederate soldiers. It is also the site of historic Blandford Church and its breathtaking Tiffany stained-glass windows.

Description: Blandford Church in Petersburg, Virginia, was used as a field hospital during the longest siege in American history. The siege of Petersburg lasted more than nine months, from June 15, 1864, to April 3, 1865. In 1901, work began to restore Blandford Church for use as a Confederate memorial chapel. The Ladies Memorial Association raised funds from each of the former Confederate states to commission stained glass windows in memory of the fallen Confederate soldiers from each state. Louis Comfort of Tiffany's studio designed the fifteen memorial windows and selected the subject and theme for each. The larger windows include the image of saints and the symbols associated with each saint.

Location: 319 South Crater Rd., Petersburg, Virginia 23803-4425

Blandford Church.

Drive the Extensive Lines West of Petersburg
Petersburg, Virginia

Why? As the siege of Petersburg dragged into the summer and fall of 1864, the opposing sides continued to move westward, building trench lines and fighting battles along the way.

Description: After the initial failure to break the Confederate lines around Petersburg, Union General Ulysses S. Grant engaged in a strategy to force a battle outside of entrenchments. For Grant, this meant pushing west of Petersburg against the Confederate right flank. Confederate General

Death in the trenches at Petersburg.

Robert E. Lee, attempting to thwart Grant's strategy, began building extensive earthworks to the west, dangerously extending his already thin lines. Although it took more than nine months, eventually Lee's lines stretched to their breaking point.

Today, much of these western lines are protected as part of Petersburg National Battlefield Park. Although the park maintains visitor centers in Petersburg, Hopewell, and Five Forks, the best way to envision the scope of the siege is to take the driving tour outlined on the park map, which is available at all three centers. The thirty-three-mile driving tour includes thirteen different sites, including Pamplin Park and interpreted sites at Reams Station, Poplar Grove National Cemetery, White Oak Road, and Hatcher's Run. The Eastern Front Visitor Center in Petersburg offers exhibits and audiovisual programs to introduce visitors to the siege of Petersburg. An audio version of the driving tour is also available for purchase. Make sure to see the huge and impressive Fort Fisher, and, for the more adventurous, walk the park's trail to Fort Welch.

Location: 5001 Siege Rd., Petersburg, Virginia 23803

Experience "Trial by Fire" at Pamplin Historical Park
Petersburg, Virginia

Why? *Pamplin Historical Park and its National Museum of the Civil War Soldier provide hands-on exhibits that will thrill children and adults alike.*

Description: Pamplin Park allows visitors to journey back in time to the Civil War era. The park sits at the epicenter of fighting on April 2, 1865—where Union forces broke through the Confederate lines around Petersburg, which led to the Confederates' evacuation of Richmond that evening. Today, Pamplin Park boasts four museums, four antebellum homes, living history venues, and shopping opportunities for history buffs. The National Museum of the Civil War Soldier, the largest museum at Pamplin, uses innovative technology to tell the story of the three million common soldiers who fought in the Civil War. The museum provides an audio player and headphones that enable you to experience the war through the words of a personal "soldier comrade." Galleries include interactive computers, videos, life-size dioramas, and more than 1,000 period relics. Most memorable is the multi-sensory battlefield simulation "Trial by Fire." This gallery re-creates the sounds and sights of battle. Troops march toward you, officers scream commands, the floor shakes, and bullets seem to whiz by your head. It is simply an unforgettable experience.

Location: 6125 Boydton Plank Rd., Petersburg, Virginia 23803

The entrance to Pamplin Historical Park.

Tour the Sailor's Creek Battlefield
Rice, Virginia

Why? *The battle of Sailor's Creek inflicted a devastating blow on the retreating Confederate army, which surrendered three days later at Appomattox.*

Description: General Robert E. Lee's ragged and outnumbered Army of Northern Virginia fled from Petersburg and Richmond in April 1865 in a desperate attempt to escape southward to North Carolina. The army's first stop on the retreat was to the Amelia courthouse, where much-needed supplies were to be waiting. However, the expected supplies were not there, and the delay waiting for their arrival enabled the Union army to catch up to Lee. On April 6, Federal soldiers, hot on the heels of a part of Lee's army, overtook them as they bogged down along Sailor's Creek. In the ensuing battle, Lee lost some 7,700 men, including eight generals captured by the enemy. Lee declared, "My God, has the Army dissolved?" The loss was a key factor in Lee's decision to surrender his army to General Ulysses S. Grant at Appomattox Court House only seventy-two hours later, bringing an end to the Civil War in Virginia. Although the spelling of the battle is not the same as that of the road on which it was fought, visit this state park for a glimpse into armies near victory and defeat.

Location: 6541 Sayler's Creek Rd., Jetersville, Virginia 23966

Sailor's Creek, Virginia.

STAND WHERE GRANT AND LEE FINALLY MET
Appomattox Courthouse National Historic Park, Virginia

Why? On April 9, 1865, a magnanimous gesture by General Ulysses S. Grant to a worthy adversary helped heal the deep wounds of a bitter civil war.

Description: On April 9, 1865, after four long years of war that had devastated much of the South and left more than 600,000 Americans dead, General Robert E. Lee surrendered the Confederate Army of Northern Virginia to General Ulysses S. Grant. Lee's surrender virtually ended the war in Virginia and fostered the surrender of the remaining Confederate armies in the field. The surrender documents were signed at the home of Wilmer and Virginia McLean in the courthouse town of Appomattox. General Lee arrived at the McLean House at about 1 p.m.; General Grant followed thirty minutes later. The terms they settled on were extremely generous to the Southern army, which helped heal the wounds of war. The Federal government would use Grant's terms as the model for the surrenders that followed. The McLean House was later used as the headquarters of Union General John Gibbon. Visitors are able to tour the house, walk the old country lanes, visit the town's other historic buildings, and see the spot where the Confederates, many of them in tears, surrendered their weapons and their shot-torn battle flags. The house itself was dismantled in 1893 for display in Washington, but plans stalled and eventually the house was carefully reconstructed on its original foundation in the 1940s.

Location: Virginia 24, Appomattox, Virginia 24522

The McLean House, Appomattox Court House.

CIVIL WAR 150 CHECKLIST

THE BASICS: *Books to Bullets*

- ❏ Hold a Minie Ball in Your Hand
- ❏ Don a Uniform or Period Dress
- ❏ Take a Bite of Hardtack
- ❏ Go to a Civil War Round Table Meeting
- ❏ Read a Bruce Catton Book
- ❏ Read and Watch *Gone With the Wind*
- ❏ See the Movie *Glory*
- ❏ Watch Ken Burns' Miniseries *The Civil War*
- ❏ Preserve a Battlefield
- ❏ Get a Kid Interested in the Civil War
- ❏ Take a Civil War Driving Tour
- ❏ Experience a Reenactment
- ❏ Pick Up a Cannonball or Shell
- ❏ Fire a Civil War Gun
- ❏ Don't Do This List Alone
- ❏ Read *Battle Cry of Freedom*
- ❏ Visit a Confederate Cemetery
- ❏ Stroll Through a National Cemetery
- ❏ Experience a Battlefield Illumination Event
- ❏ See *The Great Locomotive Chase*
- ❏ Appreciate the Crater Scene in *Cold Mountain*
- ❏ See the Flank Attack in *Gods and Generals*
- ❏ Use Your Smartphone on a Battlefield Tour
- ❏ Browse Images at the Library of Congress
- ❏ Step into 3-D Civil War Photos
- ❏ Find a Civil War Ancestor
- ❏ Climb a Battlefield Observatory
- ❏ See a Civil War Site Long Gone
- ❏ Visit a Local Civil War Monument

POINTS WEST: *Kentucky, Tennessee, Mississippi, and Beyond*

- ❏ See the Diverse Sites at Mill Springs
- ❏ Visit Kentucky's Largest Battle: Perryville
- ❏ Find Familiar Names at Lexington Cemetery
- ❏ See a Camp you Never Knew: Camp Nelson
- ❏ See Where Grant Became Famous: Fort Donelson
- ❏ Tour the Pristine National Military Park: Shiloh
- ❏ Stand Where General Albert Sidney Johnston Died
- ❏ Stand on Carnton's Porch
- ❏ See Bullet-Riddled History at the Carter House
- ❏ Learn How Chattanooga Was Defended
- ❏ See the Site with the Highest Casualty Rate—Stones River
- ❏ Visit Corinth: Besieged, Secured, and Defended
- ❏ Learn of Forrest's Wizardry at Brice's Crossroads
- ❏ See the Smallest National Civil War Park: Tupelo
- ❏ Visit the Citadel City: Vicksburg
- ❏ Walk Through the USS *Cairo* Skeleton
- ❏ "Full Speed Ahead" to Mobile Bay
- ❏ See the Last Bastion on the Mississippi: Port Hudson
- ❏ Tour Pea Ridge National Military Park
- ❏ See Abraham Lincoln's Springfield Home
- ❏ Tour the Bull Run of the West: Wilson's Creek

- ❑ See the Final Battlefield: Palmito Ranch
- ❑ Visit New Mexico's Glorieta Pass
- ❑ Visit the Westernmost Battlefield: Picacho Peak
- ❑ Explore the Drum Barracks Civil War Museum

THE COAST: *Georgia, the Carolinas, and Florida*

- ❑ See an Array of Small Arms at Chickamauga
- ❑ See Where George Thomas Became the Rock
- ❑ Drive the Atlanta Campaign
- ❑ See What the Soldiers Saw at Pickett's Mill
- ❑ Read Sam Watkins' Account at the Dead Angle
- ❑ Explore the Southern Museum
- ❑ See the Atlanta History Center's Collections
- ❑ Experience the Rotating Atlanta Cyclorama
- ❑ Visit Generals and Margaret Mitchell at Rest
- ❑ Explore the Port Columbus Civil War Naval Museum
- ❑ Tour the Notorious Andersonville Prison Site
- ❑ See the Largest Monument: Stone Mountain
- ❑ See 11-Foot-Thick Walls at Fort Pulaski
- ❑ Tour the South Carolina Confederate Relic Room
- ❑ See Fortifications of War: Fort Moultrie
- ❑ Set Sail to Fort Sumter
- ❑ See the Actual HL *Hunley* Submarine
- ❑ Spend Time in the Historic City of Charleston
- ❑ Run the Blockade to Fort Fisher
- ❑ Tour Averasboro and Bentonville Battlefields
- ❑ See the Largest Surrender: Bennett Place
- ❑ Tour a Civil War Battlefield in Florida

THE MID-ATLANTIC: *D.C. to West Virginia to Boston*

- ❑ Visit Shepherdstown and Boteler's Ford
- ❑ Stand in John Brown's Fort
- ❑ Go to Philippi and Rich Mountain
- ❑ Visit the National Museum of Civil War Medicine
- ❑ See Where Washington Was Saved: Monocacy
- ❑ Cross the Gaps in South Mountain
- ❑ Stand Inside Dunker Church
- ❑ Walk Through the Bloody Cornfield
- ❑ Stroll the Length of the Sunken Road
- ❑ Charge across Burnside's Bridge
- ❑ Feel Compassion at the Clara Barton House
- ❑ Visit the Frederick Douglass House
- ❑ Go to the National Portrait Gallery
- ❑ See the African American Civil War Memorial
- ❑ Read Eloquent Words at the Lincoln Memorial
- ❑ See Lincoln's Summer Cottage
- ❑ Visit the Sole Battle in the District: Fort Stevens
- ❑ Go into Ford's Theatre
- ❑ Follow John Wilkes Booth's Escape Route
- ❑ See Where the Armies First Met at Gettysburg
- ❑ Traverse Rocky Heights South of Gettysburg

- [ ] Stand on America's Bloodiest Piece of Property
- [ ] See Gettysburg's Important Flank: Culp's Hill
- [ ] Walk the Fields of Pickett's Charge
- [ ] See Where the Gettysburg Address Was Completed
- [ ] Visit Philadelphia's Civil War Sites
- [ ] See the 54th Massachusetts Monument

VIRGINIA: Between the Capitals

- [ ] Visit Arlington House and Cemetery
- [ ] See the Best-Preserved Capital Fort: Fort Ward
- [ ] See Ball's Bluff, a Small Battle with a Big Shadow
- [ ] Take the Henry Hill Walking Tour
- [ ] Stand in the Deep Cut at Second Manassas
- [ ] See Kelly's Ford, Where the Gallant Pelham Fell
- [ ] See the Graffiti House's Graffiti
- [ ] Stand Atop Buford's Knoll at Brandy Station
- [ ] Tour the Cedar Mountain Battlefield
- [ ] Stand in Awe at the White Oak Museum
- [ ] Visit the House and Grounds at Chatham Manor
- [ ] Stand in the Sunken Road at Fredericksburg
- [ ] See the Decisive Slaughter Pen Farm
- [ ] Tour the Chancellorsville Battlefield
- [ ] Stand at the Chancellor House Ruins
- [ ] Cross Over the River to Guinea Station
- [ ] Visit Ellwood in the Wilderness
- [ ] Walk the Clearing at Saunders Field
- [ ] Tour the Mine Run Battlefield at Payne's Farm

- [ ] Experience the Bloody Angle at Spotsylvania
- [ ] Stand in Grant's Footsteps at Massaponax
- [ ] Learn about Lee's Trap at North Anna
- [ ] Stand in the Middle Field at Third Winchester
- [ ] Tour Belle Grove and Cedar Creek Battlefield
- [ ] See the Field of Lost Shoes at New Market
- [ ] Understand Jackson's Brilliance at Port Republic
- [ ] Climb Sitlington's Hill at McDowell
- [ ] Visit Robert E. Lee's Office and Tomb
- [ ] See Stonewall Jackson's Horse
- [ ] Go In and On Fort Monroe
- [ ] See the *Monitor* Turret at the Mariners' Museum
- [ ] Tour the Confederate White House
- [ ] Visit the Confederate Arsenal at Tredegar
- [ ] See the Bloodiest of the Seven Days: Gaines' Mill
- [ ] Tour Glendale and Malvern Hill
- [ ] Contemplate Confederate Trenches at Cold Harbor
- [ ] See the Dominance of Drewry's Bluff
- [ ] Take the Trevilian Station Driving Tour
- [ ] Experience the Real Width of the James River
- [ ] Tour the Manor and Wharves at City Point
- [ ] Tour the Battlefields of Bermuda Hundred
- [ ] Gaze into the Crater
- [ ] Visit Blandford Church and Cemetery
- [ ] Drive the Extensive Lines West of Petersburg
- [ ] Experience "Trial by Fire" at Pamplin Historical Park
- [ ] Tour the Sailor's Creek Battlefield
- [ ] Stand Where Grant and Lee Finally Met

CIVIL WAR 150
QUICK REFERENCE

	Battlefield	Fort	Pristine	Bloodiest
THE BASICS				
Hold a Minie Ball in Your Hand				
Don a Uniform or Period Dress				
Take a Bite of Hardtack				
Go to a Civil War Round Table Meeting				
Read a Bruce Catton Book				
Read and Watch *Gone With the Wind*				
See the Movie *Glory*				
Watch Ken Burns' Miniseries *The Civil War*				
Preserve a Battlefield				
Get a Kid Interested in the Civil War				
Take a Civil War Driving Tour				
Experience a Reenactment				
Pick Up a Cannonball or Shell				
Fire a Civil War Gun				
Don't Do This List Alone				
Read *Battle Cry of Freedom*				
Visit a Confederate Cemetery				
Stroll Through a National Cemetery				
Experience a Battlefield Illumination Event				
See *The Great Locomotive Chase*				
Appreciate the Crater Scene in *Cold Mountain*				
See the Flank Attack in *Gods and Generals*				
Use Your Smartphone on a Battlefield Tour				
Browse Images at the Library of Congress				
Step into 3-D Civil War Photos				
Find a Civil War Ancestor				
Climb a Battlefield Observatory				
See a Civil War Site Long Gone				
Visit a Local Civil War Monument				
POINTS WEST				
See the Diverse Sites at Mill Springs	x	x		
Visit Kentucky's Largest Battlefield: Perryville	x			x

Hidden Gem	Cemetery	Hospital	Prison	Memorial	Museum	Read and Watch	Engage	Exert
							x	
							x	
							x	
							x	
						x		
						x		
						x		
						x		
							x	
							x	x
							x	
							x	
							x	
							x	
							x	
						x		
	x							
	x							
							x	
						x		
						x		
						x		
							x	
						x		
						x		
							x	
								x
							x	
			x					
x	x				x			
	x				x			x

CIVIL WAR 150
QUICK REFERENCE

	Battlefield	Fort	Pristine	Bloodiest	
Find Familiar Names at Lexington Cemetery					
See a Camp You Never Knew: Camp Nelson		x			
See Where Grant Became Famous: Fort Donelson	x	x			
Tour the Pristine National Military Park: Shiloh	x		x	x	
Stand Where General Albert Sidney Johnston Died					
Stand on Carnton's Porch	x				
See the Bullet-Riddled History at the Carter House	x			x	
Learn How Chattanooga Was Defended	x				
See the Site with the Highest Casualty Rate—Stones River	x			x	
Visit Corinth: Besieged, Secured, and Defended	x	x			
Learn of Forrest's Wizardry at Brice's Crossroads	x				
See the Smallest National Civil War Park: Tupelo	x				
Visit the Citadel City: Vicksburg	x	x			
Walk Through the USS *Cairo* Skeleton					
"Full Speed Ahead" to Mobile Bay	x	x			
See the Last Bastion on the Mississippi: Port Hudson	x	x			
Tour Pea Ridge National Military Park	x				
See Abraham Lincoln's Springfield Home					
Tour the Bull Run of the West: Wilson's Creek	x				
See the Final Battlefield: Palmito Ranch	x				
Visit New Mexico's Glorieta Pass	x				
Visit the Westernmost Battlefield: Picacho Peak	x				
Explore the Drum Barracks Civil War Museum					
THE COAST					
See an Array of Small Arms at Chickamauga					
See Where George Thomas Became the Rock	x			x	
Drive the Atlanta Campaign	x				
See What the Soldiers Saw at Pickett's Mill	x		x		
Read Sam Watkins' Account at the Dead Angle					
Explore the Southern Museum					
See the Atlanta History Center's Collections					
Experience the Rotating Atlanta Cyclorama					
Visit Generals and Margaret Mitchell at Rest	x				

Hidden Gem	Cemetery	Hospital	Prison	Memorial	Museum	Read and Watch	Engage	Exert
	X							
X	X				X		X	
	X				X			X
				X				
		X			X		X	
		X			X		X	
	X							X
	X				X			
					X		X	
	X				X			
	X				X			
					X		X	
					X			
					X		X	
X	X				X			
					X			
					X			
								X
					X			
								X
X					X		X	
					X		X	
					X		X	
	X							

CIVIL WAR 150 QUICK REFERENCE

	Battlefield	Fort	Pristine	Bloodiest	
Explore the Port Columbus Civil War Naval Museum					
Tour the Notorious Andersonville Prison Site					
See the Largest Monument: Stone Mountain					
See 11-Foot Thick Walls at Fort Pulaski	x	x			
Tour the South Carolina Confederate Relic Room					
See Fortifications of War: Fort Moultrie	x	x			
Set Sail to Fort Sumter	x	x			
See the Actual HL *Hunley* Submarine					
Spend Time in the Historic City of Charleston	x	x			
Run the Blockade to Fort Fisher	x	x			
Tour Averasboro and Bentonville Battlefields	x			x	
See the Largest Surrender: Bennett Place					
Tour a Civil War Battlefield in Florida	x				
THE MID-ATLANTIC					
Visit Shepherdstown and Boteler's Ford	x				
Stand in John Brown's Fort	x	x			
Go to Philippi and Rich Mountain	x				
Visit the National Museum of Civil War Medicine					
See Where Washington Was Saved: Monocacy	x				
Cross the Gaps in South Mountain	x				
Stand Inside Dunker Church	x				
Walk Through the Bloody Cornfield	x		x	x	
Stroll the Length of the Sunken Road	x			x	
Charge across Burnside's Bridge	x				
Feel Compassion at the Clara Barton House					
Visit the Frederick Douglass House					
Go to the National Portrait Gallery					
See the African American Civil War Memorial					
Read Eloquent Words at the Lincoln Memorial					
See Lincoln's Summer Cottage					
Visit the Sole Battle in the District: Fort Stevens	x	x			
Go into Ford's Theatre					
Follow John Wilkes Booth's Escape Route					

Hidden Gem	Cemetery	Hospital	Prison	Memorial	Museum	Read and Watch	Engage	Exert
					X		X	
	X		X					
				X				
					X			
X					X		X	
					X			
					X			
					X		X	
	X	X						
					X			
		X			X			
					X			
					X			X
								X
					X		X	
X					X			
				X				X
					X			
					X		X	
					X		X	
					X			
				X	X			
				X				
X					X		X	
					X		X	
		X			X		X	

Civil War 150 Quick Reference

	Battlefield	Fort	Pristine	Bloodiest
See Where the Armies First Met at Gettysburg	x			x
Traverse Rocky Heights South of Gettysburg	x			x
Stand on America's Bloodiest Piece of Property	x			x
See Gettysburg's Important Flank: Culp's Hill	x			
Walk the Fields of Pickett's Charge	x			x
See Where the Gettysburg Address Was Completed				
Visit Philadelphia's Civil War Sites				
See the 54th Massachusetts Monument				
VIRGINIA				
Visit Arlington House and Cemetery				
See the Best-Preserved Capital Fort: Fort Ward		x		
See Ball's Bluff, a Small Battle with a Big Shadow	x			
Take the Henry Hill Walking Tour	x			x
Stand in the Deep Cut at Second Manassas	x			x
See Kelly's Ford, Where the Gallant Pelham Fell	x			
See the Graffiti House's Graffiti				
Stand Atop Buford's Knoll at Brandy Station	x		x	
Tour the Cedar Mountain Battlefield	x			
Stand in Awe at the White Oak Museum				
Visit the House and Grounds at Chatham Manor				
Stand in the Sunken Road at Fredericksburg	x			x
See the Decisive Slaughter Pen Farm	x			x
Tour the Chancellorsville Battlefield	x			x
Stand at the Chancellor House Ruins	x			
Cross Over the River to Guinea Station				
Visit Ellwood in the Wilderness	x			
Walk the Clearing at Saunders Field	x			x
Tour the Mine Run Battlefield at Payne's Farm	x		x	
Experience the Bloody Angle at Spotsylvania	x		x	x
Stand in Grant's Footprints at Massaponax				
Learn about Lee's Trap at North Anna	x		x	
Stand in the Middle Field at Third Winchester	x			x
Tour Belle Grove and Cedar Creek Battlefield	x			x

Hidden Gem	Cemetery	Hospital	Prison	Memorial	Museum	Read and Watch	Engage	Exert
								X
								X
					X		X	
	X				X			
				X				
	X				X			
X					X			
	X							X
					X			X
				X				
					X		X	
								X
X								
X					X		X	
					X		X	
	X				X		X	
					X			
					X		X	
	X							
X								
								X
X								
X								X
X								X
		X						

Civil War 150 Quick Reference

	Battlefield	Fort	Pristine	Bloodiest	
See the Field of Lost Shoes at New Market	x				
Understand Jackson's Brilliance at Port Republic	x				
Climb Sitlington's Hill at McDowell	x		x		
Visit Robert E. Lee's Office and Tomb					
See Stonewall Jackson's Horse					
Go In and On Fort Monroe		x			
See the *Monitor* Turret at the Mariners' Museum					
Tour the Confederate White House					
Visit the Confederate Arsenal at Tredegar					
See the Bloodiest of the Seven Days: Gaines' Mill	x			x	
Tour Glendale and Malvern Hill	x				
Contemplate Confederate Trenches at Cold Harbor	x			x	
See the Dominance of Drewry's Bluff	x	x			
Take the Trevilian Station Driving Tour					
Experience the Real Width of the James River					
Tour the Manor and Wharves at City Point					
Tour the Battlefields of Bermuda Hundred	x	x			
Gaze into the Crater	x			x	
Visit Blandford Church and Cemetery					
Drive the Extensive Lines West of Petersburg	x	x			
Experience "Trial by Fire" at Pamplin Historical Park	x				
Tour the Sailor's Creek Battlefield	x		x		
Stand Where Grant and Lee Finally Met	x				

Hidden Gem	Cemetery	Hospital	Prison	Memorial	Museum	Read and Watch	Engage	Exert
					X		X	
X								
X								X
				X	X			
				X	X			
					X		X	
					X		X	
					X		X	
					X		X	
					X			
X								
								X
							X	
		X			X		X	
	X							
	X							X
					X		X	X
X								
					X		X	

INDEX

PRESERVE

The Civil War Trust is the only national nonprofit organization dedicated to preserving America's hallowed Civil War battlegrounds.

EDUCATE

The Civil War Trust is committed to educating the public about America's Civil War heritage, through interpretive walking trails and teacher programs.

ENJOY

The Civil War Trust works with government officials and other nonprofits to encourage tourists to visit and enjoy preserved Civil War battlefields.

To learn more about the Civil War and to help the Civil War Trust in its mission, visit:

CIVILWAR.ORG